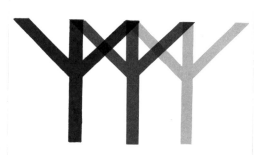

**Civic Garden Centre
Library**

BASIC BOOK OF **PRUNING**

IN THE SAME SERIES

Flower Gardening
Vegetable Growing
Rock Gardens and Pools
Chrysanthemum Growing
Rose Growing
Dahlia Growing
Decorative Shrubs
The Herbaceous Border

OTHER TITLES IN PREPARATION

BASIC BOOK OF
PRUNING

W. E. SHEWELL-COOPER
MBE, NDH, FLS, FRSL, Dip.Hort.(Wye), DLitt

BARRIE & JENKINS
COMMUNICA-EUROPA

© W. E. Shewell-Cooper 1976

First published 1976
by Barrie & Jenkins Ltd,
24 Highbury Crescent, London N5 1RX

ISBN 0 214 20165 1

Typeset, printed and bound
in Great Britain by
REDWOOD BURN LIMITED
Trowbridge & Esher

Contents

List of illustrations

Black-and-white photographs and line drawings

Acknowledgements

The author is most grateful to Mrs Alban Caroe for her excellent drawings. He would also like to thank those of his staff who assisted him in the preparation of this book, especially Mrs Jenny Kern who typed the manuscript, and Mrs Roy Johnson.

To Gweneth Johnson, CDH, FGGA,
who has been such a faithful friend and colleague over the years—with many thanks.

Preface

Give me a knife or a pair of secateurs in my hand. Put me in front of a tree or bush at the right time of the year. Arrange a number of students around me – and I'll demonstrate pruning gladly, talking at great length as I make every cut carefully and deliberately. In fact, this is the way I have taught pruning for years, and it works!

But when you come to write about pruning it isn't so easy.

One correspondent wrote to me recently, saying 'My trees never seem to be like yours!' – and she was right. I do, however, want to help my gardening friends wherever I can, so I have put pen to paper on this difficult subject.

If I have failed to put the subject across it is largely because a book or an illustration is essentially only two-dimensional, and one really needs to see a tree or shrub in the round. Fellows of The Good Gardeners' Association can come to Pruning Demonstrations at which I show how to do the various jobs. Write for particulars to the Hon. Secretary at the address below. I will always be glad of any suggestions that readers can make, and especially grateful for any drawings or photographs they have made, particularly those showing 'before and after' comparisons.

Over the last thirty years I have pruned trees and shrubs in most countries of Europe and in South Africa. It is a fascinating subject and I always long to know more. When I do, another edition must appear!

W. E. SHEWELL-COOPER

Arkley Manor,
Arkley,
South Herts.

1 Why prune at all?

Ask the man in the street why apple trees are pruned and he will say, 'to make them fruit'. This is a common fallacy today! The truth, as far as most fruit trees are concerned, is that the more you prune them (when they are young at any rate), the more you delay cropping. Pruning, therefore, cannot be said to encourage fruiting – there's far more in it than that.

Many gardeners fail to prune their shrubs at all, with the result that the plants grow far too large for the space originally allotted to them. When shrubs are in fact pruned, the reason is often to reduce their dimensions either upwards or outwards, or to thin out the branches. On most occasions, all that should be necessary is to let in plenty of light and air to ensure beautiful, thick blossom.

It is a good plan to regard pruning as a necessary evil rather than an operation that invariably does good. Of course, one of the problems connected with pruning is the creation of wounds, which may easily cause the start of disease. It is, for instance, through wounds that the silver leaf disease enters. This disease attacks plums, damsons, apples, cherries, peaches and so on. The fungi spores are constantly in the atmosphere, and can easily alight on an open wound and start trouble. Always make a good, clean, sharp cut when you prune, and treat any extensive wounds.

It is often necessary to prune in order to turn a rambling, straggling type of tree or bush into a more shapely specimen. Some are pruned, as in the case of topiary, into all kinds of shapes, such as birds, balls, animals and cork-screws. Pruning may be needed to remove a dead branch or some diseased portion of a tree or bush – branches are often broken by over-cropping or by heavy snow in winter. A tree may have got too tall and need shortening, or a bush may be growing too vigorously and thus not fruiting, in which case it requires root pruning.

Growth can always be stimulated by pruning, for, by cutting back young wood, further strong growths are encouraged and these can eventually be made to form branches. Therefore

11

pruning can give the grower the number of branches he needs
on each tree, and if he is skilled he can make these branches
develop exactly where he wants them. He can thus preserve
perfect balance by keeping the branches well spaced, and so
allow the air and sunlight to reach all parts of the tree. He can
always remove unwanted shoots with his knife or secateurs,
and he can equally well leave on the tree those growths that
seem to have the productive qualities required.

In the case of fruit tree pruning, the gardener aims to
regulate the quality of the fruit. If he leaves too many spurs
or too many branches, he may certainly have quantity, but the
fruit may not be the right colour, the right size or even the
right shape. His pruning aims to ensure that good fruit is
produced regularly year after year. Sometimes when trees are
left on their own they tend to crop biennially – a good crop
one season and nothing the next. Skilled and efficient pruning
can do much to prevent this. Pruning is also carried out to aid
fruit picking and sometimes even spraying. It is difficult to
control pests and diseases on branches that are too tall. Any
good pruner knows his power. He knows that he can make the
tree grow and develop largely as he wills, and it is his skill that
determines to a great extent the future of the tree or bush. He
knows that if he cuts back the branches of his fruit trees really
hard in the winter, the trees will produce very strong wood;
on the other hand, if he summer prunes severely he definitely
tends to check the vigour of the branch or branches.

It is possible through pruning to cause a chosen bud to
'break' and grow. This means that the spreading, drooping
type of tree may be encouraged to grow more upright, and an
extremely upright specimen may be trained so that the
branches spread out more. It is important, for instance, to keep
gooseberry branches well off the ground because the spores
which cause the disease called American gooseberry mildew
blow up from the soil. A good pruner cuts young gooseberry
shoots to an upward growing bud and when the bush has
grown large he prunes back the fruiting branches in the
winter to a point where a lateral (side) growth points upwards.

My aim in this book is to teach less experienced gardeners
to have an eye on the future. A pruner always thinks of every
cut before he makes it. He says to himself, 'What will this cut
result in?' He makes a mental note of what he thinks will
happen. The following season he watches very carefully to see
what actually does happen – and this is the way he learns.

Pruning is a craft that is best learned by practice; you must think not only about the production of wood growth, but, in the case of fruit trees, also about the crop. How is the cut you make going to affect fruit production in two years' time – or even in three or four years' time?

In pruning there is no gain without some loss. If you prune back the aerial parts of a tree and leave the roots as they are, it is obvious that when spring comes there will be many more roots than shoots. This results in more growth and increased vigour, which in its turn is the cause of smaller crops. Take care to prune with a minimum of bark injury, but see to it, too, that no dying back takes place below the actual wound. If you prune young wood, therefore, prune to just above a bud; in the case of old wood, prune to another branch lower down, so as to make sure that no 'snag' is left – snag is a short length of branch which is unlikely to be able to break out into growth owing to a lack of growth buds.

With shrubs sometimes the only pruning needed may be the removal of old flower heads: this is true of azaleas and rhododendrons. This simple type of pruning is done to stop the shrub exhausting itself in trying to produce seeds. The central main shoot of a little shrub like a fuchsia can be cut back to make branches 'break', in other words to produce side branches. In this case pruning is done to check the upward growth of the plant and to encourage a better flowering, bush-like specimen.

Prune, then, to produce the shapely tree or bush you want. Prune at the right season of the year. Have a good reason for every cut you make and never be ashamed of showing your work to another gardener. You can prune some specimens in the summer, and others in the winter. You may prune your shrubs immediately after flowering or you may root prune your trees to reduce excessive growth and to make them into fruit. Your pruning may consist of bark ringing (again for the purpose of preventing excessive vigour), but even here you will have to have a good reason, as is made quite clear in Chapter 14. Study your trees and shrubs properly, and aim to work to an ideal.

2 Tools used in pruning

Knives

It's all very well to say that a bad workman blames his tools. What the writer of the proverb ought to have said was 'A bad workman can't even do good work with good tools'! The first essential for all pruning is undoubtedly a high quality Sheffield steel knife. The blade should be kept absolutely sharp; when I am pruning I keep in my pocket a little whetstone 4 in. long, $\frac{3}{4}$ in. wide and about $\frac{1}{4}$ in. thick. It's a simple matter to spit on the whetstone or to wet it with a little water, and to sharpen the blade by rubbing the whetstone on the knife blade in a circular motion.

It's easier to prune with a knife that has a slightly curved blade because the actual operation is done by drawing the blade through the wood in a kind of slicing motion. The knife

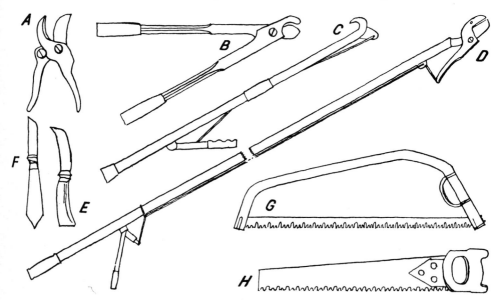

A. Secateurs   B. Guillotine   C. Long Handled Pruner   D. Long Handled Rolcut Pruner   E. Pruning Knife   F. Budding Knife G. Pruning Saw   H. Wide Toothed Pruning Saw

14

is drawn towards you and cuts through the wood at the same time. A slight curve on the blade helps the action. A knife with a stag's horn handle is good – the rough surface means it won't slip easily in your hand. The blade of this kind of knife is hinged, of course, and when shut you can safely put it in your pocket.

As a matter of fact, I much prefer to have a pruning knife that does not close because there is always a slight danger that, when working among branches high up, a pocket-knife may close accidentally. A non-clasping knife, as this is called, is firmer and steadier. After using for a number of years a knife with a blade that closes, it's apt to get loose at the rivets and then to wobble a bit. A few gardeners still use non-clasping knives today; as a rule, they carry them on a belt with the blade housed comfortably in a short leather sheath.

The pruning knife should have an overall length of about eight inches. The blade itself should be about $\frac{3}{4}$ in. wide and, say, about 4 in. long, while the handle, which is also slightly curved (it needs to be to house the blade), will be of a similar length.

Having bought a strong pruning knife with a handle that fits nicely into the palm of the hand (remember that some have larger handles than others), look for a good budding knife which can be used not only for budding but also for summer pruning. A budding knife is lighter and easier to handle in many ways, and so I use one for cutting back the side growths of vines, both under glass and in the open, for pruning the succulent growths of peaches in the summer, and for 'brutting' redcurrants in June and early July.

A budding knife may have a bone handle or one made of hard white plastic. The blade will be about 2 in. long and the handle about $4\frac{1}{4}$ in. long; the end of the handle is specially tapered and pointed so that it can be used for levering up the bark when you are budding. When fully open, the complete knife will be about $6\frac{3}{4}$ in. in length. The strong, short, pointed blade should be made of best steel, and the one I use again and again is made by Saynor of Sheffield.

Secateurs
The word secateur, of course, is a French one. Horticulturalists in France use these double-bladed scissor-like instruments largely for summer pruning. Americans disdain this name and call the tool 'clippers'. I prefer secateurs which make a cut

with a similar 'slant' to a knife and so do very little damage if the blade is kept sharp and is properly adjusted. The cut made with a pair of secateurs should be neat and clean and shouldn't cause any bruise, but whether or not you like to use secateurs for pruning apples and pears they are certainly excellent for raspberries, blackcurrants, redcurrants, loganberries and the like, and they are first-class for use with the Shewell-Cooper anglicized Lorette method of pruning, which I shall talk about in Chapter 13.

Some people recommend parrot-beaked secateurs because it is claimed they make cleaner cuts than the other kinds. In practice, however, the blades are easily strained and the beaks then cross one another and become a nuisance. Don't, therefore, be persuaded to buy secateurs of this kind. Pay as much as you can afford, and look upon the tool as a good investment. I am still using secateurs now that I bought fifteen years ago, and they are in excellent condition. Oil them with a non-corroding oil, keep them absolutely clean and always store them in a dry place when not in use.

There are two excellent types of secateurs which I can recommend.

ROLCUT These have a removable blade, which cuts on to a fairly soft piece of brass. The blade comes down gradually with a slight slant: the idea is to make a cut similar to that of a knife. Some Rolcuts are made of a very light alloy aluminium. Some, known as 'Snaggers', have a rounded top edge to the blade, and some have a diagonal top to the blade. The blades are made of steel, and to use the secateurs properly the cutting edge must be kept uppermost so that you can see the exact spot where the cut is to be made. This eliminates a lot of bruising. Never wrench the secateurs when cutting; if desired, the blade can be sharpened with a whetstone without being removed from the handle. Like all tools, keep the secateurs clean and oil them with a non-corrosive oil from time to time. All parts of the Rolcut secateurs are replaceable.

WILKINSON'S SWORD Wilkinson's offer several pruners. The Knifecut pruner is the most suitable for fruit growers: it is perfectly balanced with light alloy handles specially designed to fit the hand. It has unique double floating bearings – one holds the blades together and prevents them twisting, while the other gives the cut a smooth sliding action. The blades are rust-resisting, and a groove is provided in the holding blade to drain off the sap and stop the blades from sticking together. A very simple safety catch can easily be operated by a flick of the thumb.

The Sword pruner is cheaper and has a single floating bearing, but the other features are similar except for the safety catch. The Cutlas pruner is cheaper still – it has a simple thumb catch operated by an extra strong spring. The Pocket pruner is quite useful for summer pruning. It is very light and ideally designed for carrying in the pocket.

Each pruner works on the principle of the pruning knife. The holding blade grips the stem firmly and the keen edge-cutting blade slices through it in one single smooth cut. The action is almost effortless.

Because most people today lead busy lives and learning to use a pruning knife takes time, secateurs are very popular, especially the two kinds that have just been mentioned, because they do the very minimum of damage. The purist will say, 'Use a knife every time and you will make a very clean cut with no damage at all.' The average gardener will say, 'These modern secateurs do so little damage that I am going to use them – they are much quicker on the whole, and especially so, of course, for beginners.' Anyway, you can always use secateurs on soft fruits and cane fruits, and certainly so in the case of the anglicized Lorette pruning.

Pruning saws

There are occasions, of course, when the branch that has to be removed is much too thick for a knife or a pair of secateurs. In these circumstances you need a saw. Sometimes big branches have to be removed because they are attacked by a serious disease like canker, or maybe a tree has got too tall and its branches have to be reduced. Trees sometimes have to be 'dehorned', that is to say the branch has dropped too near the ground, so it must be sawn back to a point just above an upward growing lateral.

Pruning saws, remember, have to work satisfactorily on what is called 'green' wood and they are, therefore, quite different from the saws used by carpenters to cut through seasoned dry wood. The teeth are usually set rather wide so that they can readily saw through the green wood. Some pruning saws consist of a number of u-shaped teeth which enable the gardener to rip through the green wood quickly. Other saws have u-shaped teeth on one side and finer v-shaped teeth on the other side, the v-shaped ones being used for smaller branches, or for sawing just underneath the branches at the right spot before the main cut is made above. This is quite important because it does prevent the bark tearing later on, when the branch starts to fall. The pruner who doesn't saw below first will probably find that the weight of the branch causes the cut to crack right open when it is, say, three-quarters of the way through, and make the bark tear.

Some saws have slightly curved blades. These are usually about 12 in. long, with a four-inch-long rounded handle, slightly bevelled to make it easy to grasp. These saws are pointed and are often used when renovating a neglected orchard, for with their curve and point it is easier to get them into odd places where the branches are thick. The main cut of these saws is on the downward pull.

The curved-blade type of saw can be fitted on to a handle 4 or 5 ft long so that the pruner can saw off a branch some way up without getting on a ladder. The danger of the long-handled saw, however, is that the wound is left rough, for few gardeners will bother (after the main pruning) to put up a ladder in order to clean up the rough saw-cuts with the sharp blade of a knife. This is where a good knife comes in useful, because if a large wound is made really clean and smooth, then the cambium layer which lies just underneath the bark is able to grow out more quickly and produce a wound-healing callous to prevent the entry of disease. Immediately after cleaning up the wound and leaving it really smooth it should be painted with a thick white lead paint. This is the best substance for keeping out disease spores – far better in fact than Stockholm Tar, which used to be applied in the past. Some people purposely put a tablespoonful or two of paste driers in the white lead paint, because this then makes it dry very quickly.

There is yet another type of saw which some experts use; it really consists of a handle with a special bolt and nut at the lower end. Four different blades are provided, each one of which is slotted at the bottom end. It only takes a minute or so to fix the blade into position and to screw down the nut to fix it firmly. Blade no. 1 is very narrow indeed – about $\frac{1}{2}$ in. wide at the bottom end and $\frac{1}{8}$ in. wide at the top end. Blade no. 2 is about $\frac{3}{4}$ in. wide at the bottom end and $\frac{1}{4}$ in. wide at the top end. The other blades are similarly larger. The idea, of course, is to use the very narrow blade in places where the v of the branch of the main stem is very narrow indeed or in cases where the branches are very close together. The principle, of course, is excellent, but in practice the pruner very seldom troubles to change the blades and uses the medium size all the time!

Saws, like other tools, need looking after. They must be kept sharp and the teeth must be properly set. Most good ironmongers will service saws, but any keen do-it-yourself fan can buy a tool for setting saw teeth. The best way to use a saw is to work it evenly backwards and forwards, pressing lightly each time. It generally helps if a little oil is applied to the blade, and I usually carry in my pocket a small tin of Three-in-One oil because this oil is very suitable and the little can and squirting device are ideal for the purpose. Use a v-shaped file to keep the edges of the teeth sharp. A carpenter will show you how to use a file properly.

Long-handled pruners

If you have tall trees you will find it convenient to use a tool with a handle 6, 8 or even 10 ft long so that you can prune branches without having to use a ladder. There are two main types of long-handled pruners: the first has a pair of Rolcut secateurs fixed at the top, the knife-blade handle of which is fixed to a long, light, strong wire, at the end of which is a lever handle. When the handle is lifted, the blades of the Rolcut secateurs open; when the handle is depressed the blades close together. So the pruner opens the secateurs over the branch to be cut, and when he pulls down the handle the branch gets cut.

The second long-handled tree pruner has a special double-sided curved hook at its top end. At the lower end of this hook is a sharp blade which moves on a pivot at its base. The end of the blade is fixed to a strong wire which runs right the way down the long handle; eyes are provided to keep it in position. Oil the eyes from time to time so that the wire can slip through them easily. At the bottom of the wire is a handle which, when raised, opens the blade to its fullest extent to expose the open hook; it is this hook that goes over the branch to be pruned. The hook is then pulled down a little so that it is exactly in the position required, as well as being firm. Then the handle is pulled down. The blade passes through the branch and beyond into the slot provided by the double-sided hook. This hook-ended long-handled pruner is more popular on the whole than the Rolcut type. Generally speaking, the 8ft long-handled pruner is quite sufficient for the normal garden – the 10ft size is rather heavy to carry and tends to whip around in the wind. It takes a certain amount of skill and experience to work quickly with this pruner, as well as to ensure that the cuts are made exactly at the right point.

Some lessons and warnings about using knives
Some readers may want to use a knife regularly to get the best results. I shall therefore offer some instruction on doing the work correctly and with the minimum of effort. Take the case of the ordinary one-year-old leader (a one-year-old end growth). If this is to be pruned in the winter hold the shoot in your left hand, and put your thumb just over the bud above which you want to make a cut. Cuts should always be made just above a bud and at an angle of 45 degrees.

Place the sharp edge of the knife blade on the other side of the shoot to be pruned, exactly opposite the bud but just above it. Now make the cut with a sliding action through the shoot, turning the blade slightly upwards. It is this action that leaves the cut at an angle of 45 degrees. The idea is to draw the knife-blade towards you and simultaneously slightly to the right, which enables the blade to slip through the wood cleanly and quickly.

If the little branch to be cut is fairly thick, say ¾in. or even 1in. in diameter, quite a different technique is necessary. Grasp the branch firmly about 6in. below where the cut is to be made. With your other hand grasp the handle of your sharp pruning knife. Place the knife at the back of the point on the branch where the cut is to be made. Once again adopt a sliding motion – use the lower edge of the blade to start with and draw it through the wood so that by the time the complete cut has been made, the tip of the blade is passing through the last shred of branch. During this operation move backwards slightly so that your face is not in the way of the knife.

I must issue two warnings. The first is about where you place your thumb on the bud when you are pruning a leader. Do take care not to slice off the end of your thumb because it has been placed too far up on the bud. Secondly, I cannot stress enough how important it is to lean backwards when cutting at eye level or near to it. The point of a pruning knife can make a very nasty cut in your face.

3 Cane fruit

Many different kinds of cane fruit are grown in British gardens – raspberries, blackberries, loganberries, boysenberries, nectarberries, veitchberries and so on. With the exception perhaps of the Japanese wineberry, all these cane fruits are treated in the same way. The general aim is to cut away the cane wood which has fruited during the summer and to keep the young growth which has developed during the season. (This, of course, is not so in the case of autumn-fruiting raspberries, as will be seen later in the chapter.) Year by year, therefore, this very simple type of pruning takes place. The old wood is cut away and the young wood kept.

Some gardeners like to cut away the old wood immediately it has finished fruiting – that is to say, in the summer. They claim that as a result the developing young wood gets all the sunshine it needs and, of course, all the sap sent up by the roots. There are, however, others who say that as the leaves are the 'manufacturing centre' and because it is the foliage that produces the starches and sugar which go to make new roots and new wood, then it is better to keep all the old wood with its leaves until the foliage actually falls to the ground in the autumn.

Raspberries

If you are starting from scratch buy healthy virus-free canes and plant them in rows 5 or 6ft apart, allowing 18in. to 2ft between the canes in the rows. After planting, preferably in early November, tip the canes back to about 3ft from soil level so that they don't get blown about in the winter winds. Though years ago I used to cut the canes down to within 6in. of the ground immediately after planting, I have now discovered that better results are achieved when they are left longish during the winter and then cut down to within 8 to 10in. of the soil in March or early April when the truly live buds can be identified – and so you can cut to just above one. Cutting down the canes like this does stimulate good growth and results in fresh young canes being produced which crop well the following year.

Cane Fruits A. Boysenberry B. Loganberry C. King's Acre Berry D. Youngberry E. Japanese Wineberry F. Nectarberry G. Veitchberry

If the soil is rich in humus, and if the row is mulched with sedge peat or straw the following May, good canes may be produced during that season to a height of 6 to 8 ft. This is especially true in the case of the Malling varieties, such as Malling Promise and Malling Jewel.

There should be little pruning to do the following winter because all the canes will hopefully be new and strong. If

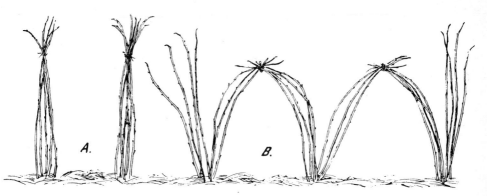

A. Canes tied in bunches ready for arching
B. Bunches tied into arches

there are any weaker canes they should be pruned back to within 1 in. of their base, and most fruit growers agree that at this early stage it pays not to have more than three strong canes per plant. It is now that the canes must be tied to wires. The tall, strong canes are not pruned until the following February or early March, when any that are over 6 ft long are cut back to about 6 ft. The idea of this tipping back, as it is called, is to encourage the fruiting spurs lower down the cane to develop. Sometimes a strong variety develops a number of side growths or laterals coming from the main cane. When this happens, the laterals should be shortened back to within 3 in. of their base at cane tipping time in early March.

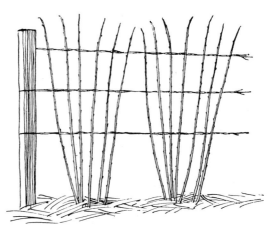

Raspberries tied up as semi-fans

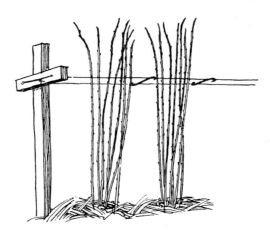

Raspberries supported by the double wire method

At the end of the first fruiting year the raspberry row should be well established, and then the normal cycle of cutting out the old wood in summer or autumn and retraining the new will be regularly carried out year after year. It isn't difficult to tell the canes that have fruited as these are rather darker coloured. Any canes that have come up in between the rows are suckers, and should be cut off carefully at their base. Where a very large number of canes develop in a clump, it is usual to reduce them down to about six and to prune those that are cut out down to within, say, $\frac{1}{2}$in. of soil level. Some people make the mistake of pruning down to within 6in. of soil level, and by doing this they leave what is called a 'dead snag' which may later become a breeding centre for diseases and pests.

There is no doubt at all that the mulching system for growing raspberries is ideal and particularly so when straw is available. Any type of straw will do but it should be put on the ground to the depth of at least 1 ft. The idea is not only to put the straw along the rows but in between the rows as well so that all the ground is covered around the crop. In this way the weeds are smothered, the moisture is kept in the soil, and you have a lovely carpet to walk on when picking the fruit. No cultivation at all is done between the rows or in the rows, so the whole operation requires very little work and yet you will have quite a heavy crop.

Some eager gardeners write and ask me whether it isn't possible to obtain some fruit in the first season after planting.

This is never advisable, but if it is absolutely necessary buy
good virus-free canes from a nursery nearby and transfer
them preferably with some soil on their roots; there should be
no time lag, and the planting should be done in soil known to
be rich in humus. In the May after planting the soil should be
mulched with medium-grade sedge peat to a depth of 1 in.,
and instead of hard pruning cut the canes down to within 3 ft
of soil level. There will be two results: first, some fruit will be
produced on the length of cane that is left, and second, some
canes will have grown to crop next year. Don't ever attempt
to adopt this plan this year, however, unless the canes that you
buy have a really good rooting system.

Autumn fruiting raspberries
At least two varieties of raspberries can be made to fruit in the
autumn – best known are the Hailshamberry and the New
Zealand strain of Lloyd George. It's usual to plant the canes
in early March and then to apply a mulch. Cutting them down
to within 8 in. of soil level in April, and the young canes that
develop as a result will crop in September and October of the
first season. I have known canes to go on cropping until late
in November when the weather was mild.

Subsequently, all the canes should be pruned down to
within 1 in. of soil level in late March each season. Then the
growth which develops during the summer will always produce
fruit in the autumn.

The Hill system
Some people like to use the Hill system, also known as the
arching over method. The principle is to plant the canes in
rows 7 ft apart and to allow 5 ft between the canes in the rows.
If the year is a good one and long canes are produced, tie them
in arches to cover the 7 ft alleyway. If, on the other hand, the
canes are too short to do this, tie them over the 5 ft alleyway.
The canes are tied into arches in March, the top of the arch
being 4 ft above soil level. It's usual to allow only four canes
to form an arch on either side.

Once all the canes have been tied to form their arches, it is
only possible to cultivate one way. But if you adopt the straw
mulching system you do not need to cultivate at all. If only
six strong canes develop per stool, train three of them to form
the arch on one side and three of them to form the arch on the
other. Allow the canes to overlap one another by about 6 in.;

one strong tie with binder twine should keep them in position without much difficulty.

The advantages of the Hill system are that the fruit is easy to pick, and the ripening berries are not shaded by the newly developing young canes. These young canes can be tied into erect bunches, as it is from these bunches that the arches are produced in the spring. Once all the fruit has been picked, or, if preferred, later in the autumn, it is a simple matter to cut all the arched canes down to soil level.

Blackberries

Blackberries produce far longer fruiting canes than raspberries, and they are also more supple. They must be supported by posts and wires, though one or two gardeners put down straw bales end to end and lay the fruiting canes on them. Normally, however, posts $2\frac{1}{2} \times 2\frac{1}{2}$ in. with L-shaped angle irons are provided at the ends of the rows. The angle irons are fitted with a stay bolted near to the top to give maximum support. The posts should be 7 ft 6 in. long and should be driven 2 ft into the ground. Impregnate the base with Cuprinol two or three days before. Wire guys (like the guy ropes used for tents) can be attached to iron pegs driven into the ground at an angle 3 ft or so behind the posts. The wires are stretched from the posts, running parallel to one another; place the bottom wire 2 ft above soil level, with the other wires 1 ft above.

Whatever pruning or training method you adopt, aim to keep the new young canes, as they develop, away from the old canes. Many years ago the young wood used to be trained under the fruiting wood as it was produced, with the result that the diease spores from the old wood invariably dropped on to the new wood and serious infection was caused. The methods described below ensure that the young canes are kept away from the old ones.

The alternate bay method

In the late autumn or early winter the old canes that have fruited are cut down to within 1 in. of soil level, and the new canes are left in position. This is possible because the new canes are on one side and the fruiting canes on the other side of the fan. The method does take up a lot of room, but it is a very simple one to adopt. The new canes are tied to their wires as they grow; they never have to be untied and tied up again as with other methods.

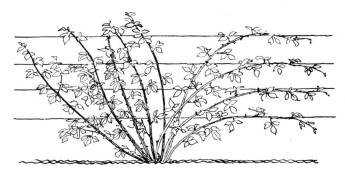

The alternative bay method. Fruiting canes (left). New canes (right)

The fan method

The idea behind this method is to train the fruiting canes out to form a graceful fan. A wide v-shaped opening is left in the centre of the fan; as the young canes grow up in the summer they are conveniently trained up the middle of the fan in the area left bare, and are then trained along the top wire. This does mean, of course, that at the end of the season the old canes are pruned down to soil level and the young canes have to be untied and tied up to form the next year's fan.

The two systems can have one or two variations. For instance, with the fan system you can train the new canes along the 6 and 7 ft wires and spread the old canes out so that they only reach the 5 ft wire. A certain amount of pruning back may be necessary in order to keep the pruning canes at 5 ft. Of course, this means you may need to reduce the actual number of canes to be trained to about six per plant. Always burn the prunings and put the ashes along the rows, for cane fruit like plenty of potash in the soil.

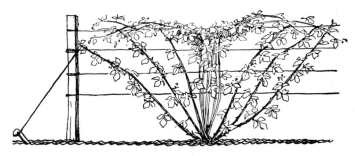

The fan method (new canes trained up the centre)

The plaiting method

Some gardeners hate pruning back canes to make them fit into any particular system, and adopt what is called the plaiting method. When the canes reach the height of the top wire they are wound in and out of it and maybe in and out of the second wire too, to form a kind of twisted pattern. If you use this method you must feed the canes well with organic manures and mulch adequately. The result, of course, is that very long canes are produced. The greater the length of cane available, generally speaking, the greater the crop.

There is one variety of blackberry – the Himalayan Berry – which grows so strongly and rampantly that it is very difficult to train and prune. The best thing to do is to allow it to have its own way – train it against a fence or even over a shed, and then instead of cutting out the old wood each year just cut back the side growths or laterals on this old wood to within 6 in. of their base. This Himalayan variety should only be planted where it is needed to form an impenetrable barrier, as the canes have very large thorns which make them difficult to manage. The thorns are in fact so large that they can tear clothes, and even the backs of the leaves have unpleasant thorns on them.

Loganberries

There is very little difference between the pruning of loganberries and the pruning of blackberries. On the whole loganberries do not produce as strong canes as blackberries, and so there isn't quite so much cutting out involved. Unfortunately some types of loganberries get badly affected by viruses and it is extremely important, therefore, to start with healthy virus-free canes.

Some gardeners have grown loganberries by training wires parallel to one another 18 in. apart and 3 ft from soil level. When the canes grow they are wrapped round and round the wires to form a kind of table. This makes the berries very easy to pick. Don't attempt to have the canes closer than 1–2 in. apart so that they can be trained round the wires. To prevent fungus spores dropping from the canes on to the new wood, train the young canes round the parallel wires to form a cable on the left-hand side of the plant or stool, and then the next year's canes are trained round and round the wires on the right-hand side of the stool.

If you don't want to adopt the table method, use any of the methods advised for blackberries. It is seldom necessary to tip them back in February or March as advised for raspberries, but it is sometimes necessary to cut poor weak canes down to soil level in the winter with the idea of encouraging better growth the following spring.

Boysenberries   The difficulty about this cane fruit is that it seldom makes enough wood in the first year after planting, and so appears disappointing. I have known it to take three years before the canes really grow as they should. Plant the canes early in November, if possible, and give them some support with a bamboo so that they do not blow about in the wind. The following mid-March, cut the canes down to within 1 ft of soil level.

It may well be that not enough canes will grow the first season after cutting down, and if this happens you will need to cut back the canes severely the following mid-March, this time to about 18 in. from soil level. If you do this, you should be rewarded with plenty of strong canes the following season. Once again it pays to mulch the ground with straw a foot deep, or else use sedge peat 1 in. deep.

Don't be under the misapprehension that the boysenberry cannot make vigorous cane growth – it can – but it is rather more particular about its soil and situation than the loganberry, and it takes much longer to settle down. But once it has become acclimatized it will grow well and crop heavily, producing enormous, delicious fruits.

Nectarberries   The nectarberry is similar to the boysenberry from the point of view of cane production, but it isn't perhaps quite so laggardly. It certainly produces the largest berries of any of the cane fruits, and these are a very dark wine shade. Prune the canes to within 15 in. of soil level about the middle of March after planting. It is unlikely you will have to do it again the following year. Sometimes, however, nectarberry canes grow very long indeed, in which case tip them back by about 12 in. in February. This will encourage fruiting lower down the cane.

Japanese wineberry   This is one of the prettiest cane fruits, because not only are the berries bright orange turning to crimson when fully ripe, but the canes themselves are orangey-scarlet also. The plants are often grown as an ornament up a post or a wall. It is usual to plant the canes 7 ft apart in November and to cut them down to within 18 in. of soil level the following March.

Prune them in very much the same way as raspberries –
cut out the old canes that have fruited in the autumn and
retain the new ones. The difference lies perhaps in the fact
that no attempt is made to reduce the number of canes per
clump. These clumps should be 7 ft away from one another
and if they are well mulched with sedge peat and fed each year
with fish manure they produce a large number of beautiful
canes.

4 Gooseberries and currants

Gooseberries, redcurrants and blackcurrants are in this chapter together because they can all be described as bush fruits. However they are all pruned quire differently, mainly because they bear their fruit in different ways. The blackcurrant, for instance, bears its fruit principally on the young wood. The redcurrant bears its fruit principally on the old wood. And the gooseberry bears fruit on the young wood as well as on short spurs on the old wood. The easiest one to prune is perhaps the redcurrant because its branches have no prickles, and it isn't difficult to form a goblet-shaped bush and then prune back the one-year-old side growths methodically each season. One thing, perhaps, that gooseberries and redcurrants do have in common is that they can suffer from a lack of potash in the soil, which makes the edges of the leaves turn brown. No amount of pruning will make up for a soil deficiency. (The answer to potash starvation, by the way, is to give plenty of wood ashes, say at $\frac{1}{2}$ lb to the square yard, as a top dressing, and hoe it in lightly.)

Gooseberries

For pruning, gooseberries can be divided into three main categories: (a) the bush tree that produces large, delicious dessert fruit, (b) the ordinary bush which produces a mass of cooking fruit, and (c) the cordon or the single-stemmed specimen which is trained against a wall, fence or wires at an angle of 45 degrees, and produces large dessert fruit. There is also a fourth type which members of the Giant Gooseberry Societies have developed, with the aim of producing large berries the size of plums.

Some gardeners plant to have a constant supply, starting, for instance, with the very early green berries grown by the thinned or regulated method; some bushes purposely spur-pruned so that really lovely dessert berries will be available; and one or two bushes with the branches trained parallel to the ground to produce immense berries for showing. Various colours of berries are available and some gardeners therefore like to have white, yellow, green and red varieties.

31

Gooseberry varieties differ in their growing habits as do the varieties of apples. Some kinds, for instance, have hanging or drooping branches. Some typical droopers are Careless, Cousen's Seedling, Leveller and London. Some varieties tend to grow upright and in this case the gardener aims, when pruning, to keep the centre of the bush open. On the other hand, when pruning a drooping variety, the leaders or one-year-old end growths are always pruned back to an upward-growing bud with the intention of keeping the branches well off the ground. Branches that trail on the ground do make it difficult to cultivate. The young shoots lying on the ground tend to throw out roots. Lastly, because the spores of the American gooseberry mildew disease blow up from the soil, the low branches easily get infected. It is fairly true to say that the further you keep the branches off the ground, the better. Incidentally, it doesn't take long for the beginner to watch the growth of any particular variety and then to decide for himself whether it is an upright-growing kind or a drooping variety.

It is always a good thing when buying gooseberry bushes to see that they are on a fairly long stem, or leg as the gardener calls it. This stem should be at least 8 or 9 in. long. If you strike your own cutting always remove the lower buds of the cutting to provide the necessary stem or leg. In the first three or four years of a bush gooseberry's life, see that good strong branches are developed to bear the fruiting laterals and the weight of the fruit. The three good buds left at the top of the cutting when it is struck should produce three good shoots evenly spaced out, forming a kind of inverted pyramid. These should be cut back the following winter by about half and to just above a bud pointing in the desired direction – usually upwards. This should mean, if all goes well, that six or seven young growths will develop, and sometimes more. The gardener then prunes back those that he wants to make into permanent branches by about half, once again to just above a bud pointing in the right direction. If at that time there are some laterals (one-year-old side growths) which tend to cross into the centre of the bush, either cut these out altogether or prune them back to within 1 in. of their base. The decision whether or not to cut the strong shoot back completely will depend on (a) its strength and (b) the direction in which it is growing. Remember that an over-strong shoot pruned back hard may easily produce two more over-strong shoots, and these will be a nuisance to have to prune next year.

One of the major problems with gooseberries is that birds have a habit of pecking out the fruit buds in the winter months. It is better, therefore, to delay pruning gooseberries until the spring because the bushes then stay thick in the winter and this may help to discourage bird attacks. There is a spider's-web-like product available called Scaraweb which doesn't take more than a few moments to apply and is very effective. Another method of keeping the birds away is to string up black cotton between the branches. The birds do not see it as easily as white cotton. They come down to peck the buds, the black cotton touches their wings, and then they are frightened and fly away.

From the third year onwards (or in the cases of poor growth, the fourth year) the method of pruning will alter. The branches should be established and now the gardener can switch to the tinned or regulated method, or to spur pruning. In both cases, however, keep a sharp lookout for suckers coming up from the roots. These are seldom any trouble if the propagation was done properly, but where live buds were left on the cuttings by mistake, root suckering is quite common. These suckers must be cut right back to their base, even if it means moving the soil and exposing the spot from which they grow. In fairness, however, I should say that some commercial fruit growers – especially on light sandy loam – prefer to have bushes without any leg at all, and they allow a number of branches to develop from the roots. They claim that this scheme is better because if one of the fungus diseases should kill the main stem, then there are always secondary stems which can take their place. In the private garden, however, it saves an infinite amount of time and trouble if all bushes are on a good leg.

The thinned or regulated method
Once the gooseberry bush is established at the end of its third year, the gardener can expect fruiting berries to be produced on the two-year-old wood as well as the one-year-old wood. Because pruning involves labour, and because the prickles or spines can scratch you, most beginners prefer the thinned system. The idea is to prune the branches as little as possible.

The pruner usually works like this: (a) he cuts away the branches that are too close to the ground, (b) he prunes back the young wood to an upward-growing bud, (c) he cuts out any dead wood there may be, (d) he cuts out the branches that are rubbing one another, (e) he thins out crowding branches so as to make certain that each one is 2 in. away from the next, (f) he aims to keep the centre of the bush open. After he has done this necessary thinning work it should be possible to get his hand in anywhere between the branches without getting it scratched.

Of course, in the fourth and fifth years of the life of the bush, it may appear necessary to cut back the leaders or one-year-old end growths by about half to a bud pointing in the desired direction. In this way good strong branches can be ensured which will satisfactorily bear the weight of the fruit later on. If a number of these leaders have to be pruned at the same time, keep their height level throughout the bush because then the sap will rise to the same point in each branch at the same time.

I am sometimes asked when the pruning of the leaders should cease and the answer, generally speaking, is when the bush has a spread of about 3 ft. At this time there should be about eighteen good branches of the desired length, and when that happens thinning out without any leader pruning is done every spring. Many people spray other fruit with a tar distillate wash in December, after pruning (because it is pointless to winter wash a branch that is going to be removed and burnt) – but gooseberries need to be sprayed with this wash in December, before pruning. Tar oil discourages birds.

Spur pruning

The bushes are pruned for the first three years to form a good strong framework as already described. The bush should be on an 8 in. leg and the three or four good shots which have developed at the end of the struck cutting are pruned back quite hard – to within 4 in. of their base – the following winter. Hopefully eight good shoots will develop: shorten these in their turn by about half a year later, making a cut just above an outward-growing bud. The exception to the rule is the Leveller variety which is often pruned by the spur method; because this variety tends to sprawl, cuts may have to be made to just above an inward-growing bud with the idea of keeping the branches growing upwards. On the whole, I find that the drooping or spreading varieties have to be cut a little harder than the more normal upward-growing kinds.

At the end of the third year, eight or nine good strong branches should have been formed, and if they have, the new lateral growths (one-year-old side growths) should be cut back in early spring to within 2 in. of their base. The leaders on each branch are then cut back by a quarter to just above a bud, if they are very strong, and back by about half if they are weak.

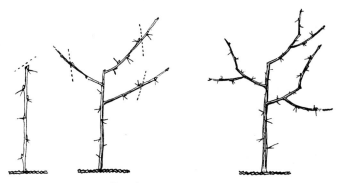

Forming a gooseberry bush

Aim to keep the tops of the branches fairly level after each pruning. Thus year after year the leader is cut back, say by half, and the laterals or side growths are pruned back to within 1 in. of their base. Each branch on a spur-trained tree, therefore, begins after a time to look like a cordon.

Not only are the spur-pruned bushes winter pruned (actually the pruning is done very late in the winter or very early in the spring), but it is usual to summer prune as well. In this case the young laterals, which of course are soft and lush in the summer, are cut back to within 5 in. of their base late in June or early in July. It is, of course, these laterals which in turn are pruned back harder.

The gardener who uses the spurred system does have more work to do both in the summer and in the late winter, but in compensation he does get bigger and better berries. It is also far easier and quicker to pick the gooseberries from nice strong branches that have grown evenly spaced in the spurred system than it is from the somewhat thicker bush on the regulated system.

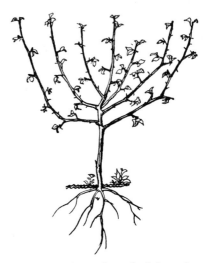

Spur pruned gooseberry bush in spring

Cordons

A cordon can be a single-stemmed branch trained against
wires attached to a fence or wall. Some nurserymen supply
dual cordons – those are bushes with two branches growing
parallel to one another – and it is possible also to have triple
cordons with three branches spaced out 6 in. apart and
growing parallel to one another also.

To form a single cordon, strike a cutting in the usual way,
leaving three good buds at the top of the cutting. At the end
of the year the most upright shoot at the end of the cutting is
selected and shortened back to within 9 in. of its base, to just
above a bud. The other two shoots or laterals are then cut
back to within 1 in. of their base. The leader or extension shoot
which has been pruned back to 9 in. should grow stronger the
following year and should be trained upwards, tied to a
bamboo so that it is absolutely straight. The two laterals or
side shoots must be watched carefully, and if they produce
sappy young growths in the summer these must be cut back
to within one leaf of their base in about the third week of July.
By concentrating on the extension shoot the sap should cause it
to grow strongly so that the following winter it can be pruned
back again by half. The laterals or side growths which
develop in the summer must be cut back in the third week of
July to within four leaves of their base, and late the following
winter they must be pruned back further to within two buds

of their base. By this method, the leader is pruned each year
and the laterals are controlled in the way already described
until they fill the space allotted to them.

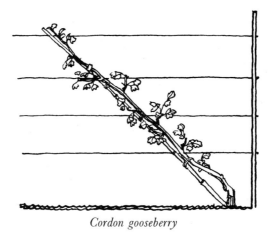

Cordon gooseberry

Generally speaking, the cordons are planted at an angle of
45 degrees because (a) this will make them take longer to
reach the top of the wire or fence, and (b) at this angle there is
a slight check in the flow of the sap, which encourages fruiting.
Some gardeners like to plant the cordons upright to start with,
and then after a year bend them and train them at an angle of
45 degrees. This, they say, checks the flow of the sap better
than by planting them on the slant in the first place.

After seven or eight years the cordons can be untied to
reduce the angle at which they are growing from 45 to 30
degrees. This, of course, allows them to grow even longer
before they reach the top of the wire, wall or fence. After many
years I have discovered that it seldom pays to have the cordons
longer than 7 ft. When gardeners grow them 8 or 9 ft long the
lower spurs suffer at the expense of those at the upper end of
the cordons and in consequence these fail to fruit.

If you want to produce your own dual cordons you must, in
the early stages of the life of the plant, cut away the central
shoot entirely and then take the two next side shoots and prune
them to within 5 in. of their base. The aim once again is to
have the tops level so that the shoots that result are of a similar
length and strength. These two shoots are then pruned back
by about half, and gradually each one of them is built up year
after year as if they were single cordons. It isn't a difficult

matter to select three equally spaced shoots, prune them equally hard, and thus form a triple shoot. On the whole, however, it is really better for the amateur to allow the nurseryman to develop the dual or triple cordons for, say, three years so that they are bought already established.

Pruning for show

Those who grow gooseberries for exhibition and show purposes aim to have the branches parallel to the roots. When the planting is carried out the roots are spaced out very evenly indeed so that they really do radiate from the main stem. Furthermore, the plan is to see that they are all, as far as possible, exactly at the same depth as one another and this usually means no deeper than 4 or 5 in. The branches are then trained very carefully so that they run parallel to the soil. Specially strong wires with hooks on the end must be used so that the branches can be pulled down to the right level, while other wires with a v at the top keep any branches that tend to droop up to the right level.

The main stem of the bush should be 15 to 18 in. long so that the branches are raised well above soil level. Seven main shoots on each bush should be trained to radiate out equally from the main stem, and it is in this way that the stems are kept at an even balance with the roots below.

Each year cut back to within $\frac{1}{2}$ in. of its base the one-year-old branch that has cropped the previous season. Then choose one or two strong laterals that have been produced during the season and train them out, using wires, so that they form a flat table with all the branches running parallel to the soil. It is here where the u's or v's on the wires come into play as well as the hooks. I have often found it necessary to use between 20 and 24 of these wire hooks and v's to each bush. Some varieties are particularly suitable for this method of pruning, and they are Lord Derby, a red; Stockwell and Surprise, both green; Leveller, a yellow; and London, another red. Sometimes, when pruning in the winter, it will be found that the young tips of the branches have been ruined by aphides or mildew disease. The tips may be twisted, brown and malformed: if so, they should be pruned off carefully and burnt. The bushes will need careful spraying in future.

Redcurrants Redcurrants are either grown as bushes or as cordons, and in the latter case they are usually planted against a north wall.

This is quite a profitable way of using a shady spot in the garden. When the currant is to be trained as a cordon it is treated in a similar manner as described for gooseberries, but the way a redcurrant bush is trained is peculiar to this fruit. The cutting back is struck either by the gardener or in the nursery and must be trimmed of its basal buds. The aim in the case of the bush is to have a good leg 6 in. long and it is necessary, therefore, to strike a long cutting.

At the end of the first year the three buds at the top of the cutting will hopefully have grown well and will be about 8 or 9 in. long, but whether they are of this length or not they must be cut back the first winter to within 4 in. of their base. The cuts must be made to just above an outward-pointing bud at an angle of about 45 degrees. The gardener aims by this and by the cuts made later in the winter to produce a perfect goblet-shaped bush.

As the result of this early, very hard pruning, numbers of strong growths should develop. Some will be good leaders pointing upwards while others may be laterals and side growths growing outwards. Wait until all the leaves have fallen before pruning the leaders or end growths back by about half, to just above a leader or upward pointing bud; cut the side growths back to within 1 in. of their base. This method of pruning is used for the first four winters after the bush is planted, and this is how you produce really strong branches to form the goblet.

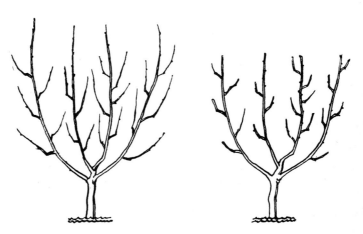

A spurred tree before and after pruning. In this case the leaders have been pruned hard back

After five years it will be possible to stop pruning the leaders or one-year-old end growths quite so hard, as the branches will have been formed. The idea now is to allow them to extend a little further each year, and so the pruning back will be reduced by about a quarter. The laterals, however, will continue to be pruned back hard and so the ideal goblet-shaped bush will be produced which will allow plenty of light and air to get to the centre. Each branch is pruned as though it were a cordon, and it is on the spurs (as they are called) that the heavy crops of berries will be produced.

The gardner's aim is to have the bushes about 6 ft apart and each bush should have about nine branches. Redcurrants should be planted 5 ft-square in the normal garden, though if the soil is sandy and poor, 4 ft-square may do. One variety, Fay's Prolific, never grows very strongly and may be planted 4 ft-square even on strong soil. Watch out with Fay's for blind or dead buds. It is important to make a cut just above a bud that is alive and will grow out in consequence the following spring. It's no good pruning back to just above a dead bud! Weak-growing varieties need pruning harder. It is just a question of altering the pruning to suit the variety.

I have, on occasions, left unpruned any side growths or laterals on the branches that are not more than 4 in. long. These will often bear a number of bunches of redcurrants in consequence. This cannot be done, incidentally, until the bushes are over six years of age. If the laterals are left in this way, they must in their turn be pruned to within 1 in. of their base the following winter.

As with gooseberries, redcurrants can send up suckers from their roots. These strong young growths can be a nuisance. They occur when the cutting has not been properly prepared, and they must be cut out right to their base in November. There is a disease called coral spot which produces small blisters, usually twice as large as a pinhead, on the stem or branch. If the main stem of a redcurrant bush is killed by this disease a sucker is useful as a replacement, and in this case the bush has to be 'built up' once more from the beginning.

Summer pruning or brutting

In addition to the normal winter pruning already advised, redcurrants need summer pruning, known as 'brutting'. Instead of cutting the laterals with the sharp edge of the knife blade, break them off with the back of a knife, thus leaving a rough edge. All these laterals are thus reduced in June to within 6 in. of their base. The result, of course, is that sunlight and air are let into the bush and the fruit ripens better. The production of more fruit buds is encouraged as the result of this seemingly drastic operation.

Three-year-old redcurrant before pruning

Three-year-old redcurrant after pruning

Brutted

Never reduce the end growths or leaders when brutting. Though normally brutting is done in June, the idea is to do the work the moment the redcurrants begin to ripen. The reason the shoots are broken off in this way instead of being cut off cleanly with the knife is to prevent secondary growth taking place – which would, of course, just waste sap. The summer prunings can be put on the compost heap; if sprinkled with an activator like fish manure they will rot down quickly and produce good compost.

Cordons

Redcurrants can also be grown successfully as cordons. Single, double and even triple cordons are available, and these are trained up wire fences or tied to wires stretched tightly against a wall or fence. It is usual to plant the cordons about 2ft apart, at an angle of 45 degrees. The alternative, as with gooseberries, is to plant them upright the first year and then train them at an angle of 45 degrees the second year; after they have been in eight or nine years they may be untied and tied in again at an angle of 30 degrees.

Redcurrants grown as cordons are on the whole treated similarly to those grown as bushes. The end growth or leader is cut back by about half each winter to just above a bud pointing in the desired direction. The one-year-old side growths are pruned back at the same time to within 1 in. of their base. Pruning is usually done in November so that winter washing can be done in December.

As far as summer pruning is concerned, all the young laterals are brutted off by half with the back of the knife blade the moment the berries start to turn colour.

Half-standards

Some people like to grow their redcurrants as half-standards instead of having a stem about 8in. tall. The nurseryman allows the top growth only to develop, as advised for cordons, until it reaches a height of 3ft. He then prunes back the main stem to make it break out and produce branches. Meanwhile, as this main stem is developing, the laterals that grow out of the side are pruned back to within 1 in. of their base and so eventually you get what may be described as a redcurrant tree on a 3ft stem, and yet all the way up this main stem fruit is borne on short spurs.

I have seen a half-standard redcurrant planted purposely

in the corner of a herbaceous border and it looked fascinating and most unusual in the summer, covered from top to bottom with glistening crimson bunches of berries. Most nurserymen who specialize in fruit will be only too pleased to supply red-currants trained in this way. They are, of course, more expensive than ordinary bushes, but they crop very heavily indeed and they look most attractive.

Blackcurrants This is a totally different kind of bush from either the goose-berry or redcurrant. Whereas these two should be grown on a stem or a leg, it is important for blackcurrants to have their branches rising direct from ground level. The reason, of course, is because the blackcurrant produces its fruit on the wood produced the previous year, usually called the young wood. The gardener, therefore, says that he grows the blackcurrant as a stool.

It is usual to buy a blackcurrant bush as a two-year-old, and the moment this young bush has been planted all the branches should be cut down to within 2 in. of soil level. It is never advisable to try to make these branches produce fruit the first season. Having pruned this young bush drastically, the young wood that is produced during the following summer will fruit well the season after, but if no pruning is done at all that winter the danger is that all the branches will be 'old' the following year and so will not crop. It is therefore quite a good idea to sacrifice one of the branches by cutting it down quite hard. After this remove, say, two or three branches bodily each November, for this hard pruning will force the bush into nice strong growth.

After the first five years it is best to cut out not more than a third of the branches each season. In this way, not only is the bush kept growing vigorously but there is always enough young wood to carry a good crop of fruit. During experiments that I carried out for some ten years, however, I discovered that it is quite easy to over-prune blackcurrant bushes after the sixth year. The general recommendation, as a result of the research, is that branches that tend to fall down to soil level should be removed and branches right in the middle of the bush should be cut out, but no attempt should be made to remove all the old wood as some books advise. If you winter prune like this the branches will be evenly spaced at 8 in. apart, each branch carrying some length of young wood on it. In this way there will be enough leaves present to manu-

Three-year-old blackcurrant before pruning

Three-year-old blackcurrant after pruning

facture the elaborated sap to feed the berries and the wood, and in addition give sufficient room to make for ease of picking and spraying.

Those who are new to blackcurrant pruning are sometimes mystified by the instructions given to cut out the old wood each winter and leave in the new. They see that there is some young wood growing on the old wood and they are hesitant, therefore, about pruning out the old branch. Of course, the old wood will have some young shoots on it, but if the aim is to cut out a couple of the oldest branches each year, then the bush can be kept vigorous. Fortunately pruning in the case of a blackcurrant is easy, for it's not necessary to prune back to any particular bud. There are what are termed 'pin' buds on almost any part of the old wood, and so it is possible to cut back to any point and find that shoots are sent out quite naturally.

Note that no leader pruning is done at all in the case of blackcurrants. The extension shoots, therefore, are not cut back in any way. Furthermore, no attempt is made to prune back any of the laterals as in the case of redcurrants. All the young growths are left at full length. It is entirely a renewal method of pruning year after year.

There is only one serious word of warning to be made – in respect of a virus disease known as reversion, which prevents the bushes from cropping. Any infected bushes must be burnt carefully, for when pruning it is possible to carry the virus on the blade of the knife.

5 Nuts and figs

Edible chestnut trees grow so large that they are far more suitable for forests than gardens. They are generally planted and then left alone. I shall therefore not deal with them here. In the case of almonds, a number of species that are grown as flowering trees do produce edible nuts. The trees are almost always left to grow naturally, but a small section of this chapter is devoted to them. The three principal nuts grown in Britain are cobnuts, filberts and walnuts; it is to these three trees, and to figs, that most of the chapter is devoted.

Cobnuts and filberts

Cobnuts and filberts are very similar, and in fact the variety called Kentish Cob is often known as Lambert's Filbert. Cobs have nice fat longish nuts with outer husks that are only slightly longer than the nuts themselves. Filberts, as a rule, have husks considerably longer than the nuts. That is the main way of differentiating between them.

Experts agree that these nuts are best grown on bushes which are trained to form an open cup shape. The bushes should have stems or legs about 2 ft high and there should be six good main branches as a start. So buy a two-year-old nut bush, which need have only three main branches: if these are cut back by half early in the spring after planting, the right number of additional branches should develop.

The following winter the leaders or one-year-old end growths will again be pruned back by half to just above an outward pointing bud. The year after, prune in a similar way and so on for four years or so until a basin-shaped bush is formed. Some people continue pruning back the extension shoots for six years, and thus form good strong main branches, though very slowly.

Of course, if the leaders are cut hard back they will not only produce further strong leaders but strong-growing laterals as well; the strongest of these, if they are in the right position, can be treated as leaders and thus gradually the branches will be increased from six to fifteen, each branch radiating from the main trunk to help from the perfect basin. The unwanted laterals can be pruned back to within 3 in. of their base with the idea of encouraging them to form fruiting spurs.

This hard pruning back of the leaders and formation of the branches can be kept up until the tree has grown to a height of 6 or 7 ft. From then on either prune the leaders back to within ½ in. of their base, or cut them out altogether. It is important to cut back all the suckers coming up from the roots right the way down to their base, or, if possible, pull them up in the summer when they first appear or at least when they can be easily grasped.

With most fruits the main pruning is carried out in November, and summer pruning is done in about July. However nuts prefer to be pruned as late in the season as possible, so that while the laterals are being cut back the pollen from the male catkins can fall on to the little female flowers. This generally means that the laterals are best pruned early in March.

The male flowers or catkins are borne on the previous season's longish, straight wood. The female flowers – tiny, reddish-mauve, brush-like blossoms – are borne on short thin laterals which generally look rather spindly. Female blossoms are also sometimes found at the base of stronger young wood. Never, therefore, cut back the older spindly wood, but do prune back to within 3 in. of their base the stronger laterals bearing the long tassel-like catkins. These catkins should be opening out and the powdery pollen should in consequence be flying about in the air. Some of it will automatically fall on the female flowers and fertilize them.

Thus we can say that the stronger laterals should be pruned back and if, as the tree gets older, wood is present that has borne heavily the previous year, this may be cut back to four buds also.

Cobnuts and filberts are also pruned or 'brutted' in the summer in a similar manner to redcurrants. The lateral growths are broken off, with the back of the blade of a strong knife, to half their length. The intention is to let light and air into the centre of the tree to enable the flower buds to ripen up better the following season. It is these brutted laterals, by the way, that should be shortened back to within 3 in. of their base in the winter.

All kinds of methods have been adopted to try to form the perfect cup-shaped bush. For instance, I have known some gardeners to place a child's large wooden hoop in the centre of the bush and carefully tie all the branches to it. Usually the hoop is used in the fourth year and is removed at the end of the ninth year when the bush has been trained to correct shape. Other nut growers drive in 6-ft-long chestnut posts, one to each branch. They they pull the branch down to the right level and tie it to the post. Many years ago they used posts 3 ft long; having driven most of each post into the soil, they then tied a branch to the top of its particular post with a piece of rope. As the tree grew and the branches needed to be opened out to form a basin, they were gradually pulled down. Few people will bother to be as fussy these days.

When the bush has got to the right height (remember that you don't want the branches so long that they make picking difficult), the leader can be pruned back in early August. This summer pruning discourages further growth, of course, far more than winter pruning.

At any point in the lifespan of a nut bush – especially, for instance, after it is twelve years old – it is possible to saw one or more of the branches back to a point just above some well-placed growth lower down, and so turn this growth into a leader. This is known as dehorning. By replacing very old branches with newer ones it revitalizes the tree. Many years ago it was common not to prune a well-placed young cobnut shoot near the base of the branch up to say the tenth year – and again not to prune it in the summer so that it would grow on to form a young branch trained to run parallel to the older one; having been grown on for a year or two the older branch would be sawn off to a point just above where the new growth started. In that way the gardener prepared his new branch a few years before cutting the old branch away.

Many people have to take over neglected gardens. The tall nut bushes found in these places are known as 'runaway' nuts. Little can be done to improve the cropping of a bush of this kind. One or two branches can be thinned out, suckers coming up from the roots can be cut off, and if you like you can try layering some of the lower branches, particularly if they are no more than two or three years old. In this way you can produce a new nut bush which can be trained properly. As nut bushes can live to a very great age, do take care of them.

Walnuts

Most British walnut trees are grown as standards. They were planted many years ago and were regarded as forest trees. These large trees need little or no pruning apart from sawing out dead, crossing or rubbing branches.

It is best to prune walnuts early in August, and any big wounds should always be cleaned up with the sharp blade of a knife before being coated with a thick white lead paint. For the first few years after a standard is planted, it helps the main stem to thicken if a number of side shoots are allowed to grow. Most people like to trim off laterals growing on the main stem because they look untidy. But it is in fact far better to leave them alone during the first four or five years; if they grow longer than about 9 in. they may be summer pruned back to 9 in. in August.

For the first four years the leaders at the head of each standard should be pruned back by about half and any crossing or rubbing laterals may be pruned back a little. After four years, however, it is usual to leave the tree alone, apart from just a little thinning out in August to prevent rubbing and crossing.

Recently, people have started to grow walnuts as bush trees and to concentrate on varieties which produce their catkins early. Two that have given good results as bushes are Franquette and Mayette. Bush walnuts can of course be kept manageable in the average garden.

Trees of two or three years of age should be bought for planting in November. The following March the one-year-old leaders should be cut back by a quarter to just above a bud. Do take great care to keep the tops of the branches level.

After this first season it is advisable to do all the pruning in the summer. Tackle leaders, for instance, in the early summer when the growing shoots are succulent and when not more than six leaves have formed. All you need then is a pair of scissors or even a long thumbnail to pinch out or 'stop' the young growth. The buds lying below should then turn into fruit buds. This is the method adopted to make sure the bush does not grow too large.

As the tree gets older, male catkins will start to be produced on the weaker shoots. Don't be tempted to stop or pinch these back, because the male pollen is badly needed. The first lot of pinching back, as I have mentioned, is done early in the summer, but actually it is possible to pinch back the shoots at any time in the growing season.

Summer pruning is imperative because winter pruning invariably makes the wood die back and rot. Experiments have shown that it is safer not to prune walnuts in March, despite what some writers have said. March pruning may result in bad bleeding. My own unbroken rule is never to prune my walnuts at any time between Christmas and May. Furthermore, it is better when pinching back not to remove more than about ½ in. of the tip. This, as you will see, is not summer pruning as some people think of it.

Of course, in the summer it is possible to do a certain amount of centre thinning to let in light and air. Trees that persist in growing too vigorously can be given a serious check if they are lifted in October for replanting in the same spot. This lifting and replanting is equivalent in effect to root pruning.

Examine the trees each May after the leaves have opened out, and if any of the branches have died during the winter cut them out and burn them. Keep the trees symmetrical when pinching back – remember that this stopping will help to encourage the growth of short lateral shoots which will tend to fruit the following year. Never encourage strong shoots in walnuts. Make sure that the trees grow very slowly, and encourage them to produce a large number of short fruiting spurs bearing both catkins and nutlets.

Figs

The main thing to remember about the fig is that you musn't attempt to grow it in good soil. It always does its best in very poor land, preferably rocky and stony. Most British figs fail because they are treated too kindly. Root pruning is therefore likely to be far more important than any form of branch pruning. Fortunately, a fig will stand almost any kind of pruning, but this means that the beginner often over-prunes, resulting in rank growth with little fruit.

In Britain, figs are often grown against walls or fences because they give the trees the extra warmth and protection that they like. If you grow them like this you must aim to produce fan-shaped trees which you can tie carefully to the wires. It is usual to buy a tree two or three years old, for November planting. Next March the branches are cut back to within 6 in. of their base to just above a bud. The growths that develop as the result of this hard pruning must then be examined carefully the following winter to decide on the number of branches to be kept. In all probability there will be about five or six strong ones, which can be spread out fanwise and tied to the wires attached to the fence or wall. Any unwanted growths will be pruned back to within two buds of their base, and the laterals which develop as a result will be stopped in the summer when they have produced six or seven leaves.

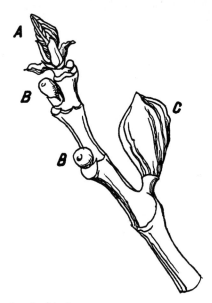

A. *Growing leaf bud*
B. *Embryo fruits*
C. *Last year's late summer fruit, withered and unripened*

This stopping is done by pinching out the growing point while it is still young and tender. Use a pair of scissors or the nails of your thumb and forefinger. It will not be long before other laterals develop, and those that are needed can be tied in to cover the space allotted, each one being stopped in the summer as and when necessary. Any growths, however, that are not wanted at all in the summer can be cut back to within one leaf of their base.

In the second year after planting, the leaders should be cut back by about half to just above a bud, but the laterals should not be touched since they should already have been dealt with in the summer. Pruning the leaders makes them strong: tie them to the wires as they develop. After the first five years, winter pruning should be unnecessary and the fan-trained tree can be left to develop quite naturally. After eight or nine years, however, there will probably be some wood to be cut out – there is always a tendency for long lengths of bare wood to appear if cutting out is not done from time to time.

Whatever fruit trees you grow, you must know where the fruits are borne, for this has a great bearing on the way the pruning is carried out. Figs are borne on the properly ripened

wood produced the previous year. Aim, therefore, at producing sturdy short-jointed growths which can get plenty of
sun to help them ripen. The main object of pruning an old-
established tree is to prevent overcrowding and to ensure that
enough sturdy short-jointed shoots are produced. Cut out about
30 per cent of the wood each November – it is often necessary
to saw down old branches almost to their base. This has proved
more effective than trying to cut away a number of widely
distributed branches all over the fan. Fortunately it is possible
to make cuts on almost any part of a fig tree, because dormant
buds seem to break out anywhere.

During the summer watch the production of side growths
and prune back any that seem to need it. Sometimes strong
lateral shoots are produced which are not needed for replacement: check these by pruning them at the tips when they are
8 in. long. It is always necessary, by the way, to cut back any
suckers growing up from the roots – tackle these in the summer
too.

Figs are winter pruned as soon as possible after the leaves
have fallen, for wounds heal quite quickly at that time.
Remember that it isn't difficult for a fan-trained fig to spread
about 35 ft wide and 15 ft high. Provide wires at a distance of
18 in. from each other, and 3 in. away from the wall or fence.
Tie the branches to wires as they grow. The fruiting wood
should be distributed about 8 or 9 in. apart all over the area
covered by the tree.

Winter pruning is designed to remove unwanted old or new
wood. Summer pruning, which is carried out in two stages,
the first in early June, aims at removing shoots growing at
right-angles to the wall or fence, which makes them difficult
to tie in. This breast wood, as it is called, is cut back hard to
its base. The second 'summer pruning' is done at the beginning
of September, when laterals can be cut back to their six leaves
with the idea of encouraging fruit buds to form – buds which
will produce flowers and fruit the following season. If the
pruning is done any earlier the buds may well have become
too soft to survive winter frosts. Always aim, therefore, to get
the tree to produce by the late autumn immature fruits no
larger than a pea: these will live through the winter and then,
after flowering, will plump up the late following spring to
produce large, luscious figs that summer.

Up to the tenth year of the fig's life you can allow one good
leader – that is to say one end growth or extension growth –

to develop from the end of each branch. A secondary shoot can also be allowed to develop from the base of this branch; it can be used as a replacement later on if necessary.

Bush figs

If you want to grow a fig as a bush, plant it in a warm sunny spot where it will have plenty of growing room. The soil should be very poor and nothing should be done to encourage the fig to grow stronger – for instance it is better not to water it much in the summer. For the first five years after planting, cut back the leaders by about half to just above a bud, and leave the laterals alone. But do cut back any that have got so long that they cross or rub other shoots. After the sixth year the fig can be left well alone, except, of course, to cut out a branch here and there if the bush appears to be too thick. Do this the moment the leaves have fallen.

Root pruning

Figs normally grow in very poor soil in Mediterranean countries. They put up with stony land and the reason they crop heavily is their great desire to reproduce themselves. Because they are starving they are only able to develop short growths and, of course, it is these that produce the fruit. In Britain, therefore, it is often necessary to root prune. For a fan-trained tree, make a half circle with a 5-ft radius taking the trunk as the centre. Dig a trench along that half circle at least 2 ft deep, and cut off all the roots you encounter with a sharpened spade, pushing it down into the soil as deeply as possible.

Some fig growers root prune their trees every four years with a half circle only 4 ft away from the main trunk. If you are growing bush figs, of course, you must root prune from a complete circle around the tree. Root pruning should be done either in early November when the leaves have fallen, or at the end of February if the ground is open.

6 Plums and cherries

One of the great problems with plums and cherries is that the wounds created by winter pruning tend to let in the spores of the silver leaf disease, *sterium purpurium*. You can of course paint the wounds with a thick white lead paint to prevent the spores entering, but this makes extra work and costs money. It is better to try and do all your pruning in the summer, for then the rising sap pushes away any spores that land on the cut surfaces. Also large wounds made with a saw and cleaned up afterwards with a sharp knife heal best in the dry summer months.

Plums

Plums, either standards or half-standards, are often best left unpruned for the first two years. Each February for the first four or five years dried blood should be given at 3 oz to the square yard all around the trees for 3 ft or so, with the idea of encouraging the branches to grow well. If in the first two summers you notice young wood growing into the centre of the tree, it may be advisable to prune out a side growth or two to prevent any wood crossing or rubbing. (The latter term refers to branches, however young, which are so close together that they rub one another when the wind blows.)

Plums (and damsons too for that matter) produce their fruit buds quite naturally on short spurs. It is not necessary, therefore, as in the case of apples, to cut back the young side growths in the winter to produce fruiting spurs. The leaders, or one-year-old extension growths at the ends of the branches, may be cut back by about half to just above a bud: this will cause another strong leader to be produced the following season. It is the pruning of the leaders after the first two years that helps to build up a strong framework on which the fruiting laterals can be borne. This regular leader pruning for, say, six years after the first two years, is very necessary, especially in the case of heavy cropping varieties like Victoria, Czar and Pershore. If heavy croppers are not pruned hard in the early stages the branches are apt to break down later on when a heavy crop is produced.

54

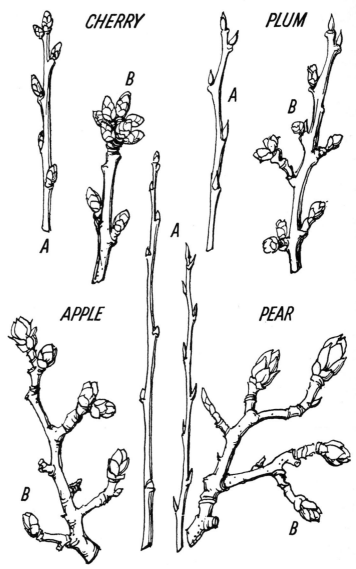

A. Leaf buds   B. Fruit buds
Typical one-year-old shoots and three-year-old spurs. Note the
difference between leaf buds and fruit buds

One of the problems about writing on pruning instead of demonstrating it is that one cannot show the exceptions to the rule. For instance, in cases where the soil is rich in organic matter, having been manured with well-rotted compost for a number of years, and where the purchased trees have been budded or grafted on to a very vigorous stock, it may be difficult to bring certain varieties into fruit early enough if the trees are hard pruned in the early years.

Talk to your nurseryman about the varieties you are buying: find out if they are strong growers, and ask him what stock they have been budded on. If, for instance, you are buying Giant Prume, Monarch or Belle de Louvain, it is better not to prune them hard after the first two years. Leader prune them in the first March (after, say, planting in November) and again in the following March, and then leave the trees alone, apart from a little thinning out of the unwanted branches in the summer.

Some varieties, if left alone, have an upright habit of growth. When you cut the leaders always make your cut just above an outward pointing bud. The idea, of course, is to ensure that the next leader grows outwards rather than inwards. Among those that I have found to grow upright naturally are President, Monarch, Czar, Blaisden Red, Gisbourne's Prolific and Belle de Louvain. Again, it would be sensible to ask the nurseryman from whom the trees are bought whether the growth is upright or spreading. New varieties are always being introduced and he should know about them.

Other varieties tend naturally to spread themselves out, and their branches droop to the ground. Varieties like this have their leaders (after the first three or four years) carefully pruned to an upward pointing bud. The idea is to make the resultant new leader grow upwards and prevent the tree from drooping. Varieties in this category include Victoria, Warwickshire Drooper, Early Laxton, Bountiful, Purple Pershore, River's Early Prolific and the Merryweather damson.

When a plum tree is, say, seven or eight years old, only a little pruning should be necessary. Good, strong branches ought by then to have been formed; there should be plenty of naturally formed fruit spurs; and the tree will undoubtedly be quite tall enough from the point of view of easy spraying and pruning. You will therefore need to cut back the one-year-old growths to discourage further strong extension growth. In the summer all you will need to do is cut back any crossing or rubbing branches, and remove entirely any young branch that may be filling up the centre of the tree, preventing the fruit buds forming and maybe the plums from getting all the sunlight they need. Any broken branches, of course, must be sawn back to a point where there is healthy growth developing in the right direction. Any suckers coming up from the roots at the base of the tree must be traced to their source and cut back there. This will undoubtedly involve digging out some of the soil.

If you take over a garden containing plum trees producing quantities of rank unfruitful growth, it is useless to prune these hard back in an attempt to force them into fruiting. Severe pruning like this only aggravates the conditions and further vigorous growth will inevitably result. A tree developing in this way should be left alone to settle down to fruiting naturally, and in fact the less it is pruned, the sooner it will come into cropping. Once it is cropping well some thinning out of the branches may be done in the summer.

Fan-trained trees

Many gardeners like to grow their plums on walls or fences. They usually buy fan-trained specimens from a nurseryman and then train the branches out carefully like sunrays, tying them with tarred string to the wires they have fixed up. If the planting is done in November – and early winter planting is best – then it should be possible to reduce the leaders on each branch by half. After this, aim to conserve most of the young growths that develop during the summer and tie them back to the wires while they are young and pliable. If, however, some laterals develop at right-angles to the wall or fence, and so are naturally difficult to tie back, prune them back in late July to within six leaves of their base.

To save money you may prefer to buy a one-year-old plum tree from a nurseryman with the idea of planting this in the spot where you propose to have fan-trained trees. If planted in November, cut it back to within 6in. of its base (that is to say to within 6in. from the point at which it was budded by the nurseryman). Make this cut just above a bud. In the spring, the buds on this 6in. length will break into growth; while they are young and, say, no longer than an inch or so, all but the two strongest should be removed with your thumb and forefinger. The two that remain should then grow well. When the upper one of the two is 18in. long, the main stem above should be pruned back to just above this growth at an angle of about 45 degrees. The two branches should then be trained at an angle of 45 degrees to one another. Tie bamboos to the wires to form a v, and tie the laterals to these with raffia. This keeps them absolutely straight. In the winter these two branches should be cut back hard to within 6 in. of their base just above a bud. As the result of this hard pruning, four branches should develop on each side of the two side branches; if there should be more than four, reduce them to four when they are 1 in. long. These in their turn are pruned back the following winter to within, say, 18 in. of their base. By this means all the necessary branches gradually produced, are trained out carefully in a fan shape.

You can also use bamboos tied to the wires first, to look like sunrays. Then as the laterals develop on the branches they can be tied to the bamboos and you can be sure your tree will adopt a regular shape. After the fifth year remove the bamboos and tie the branches to the wires.

After this period the general pruning may alter, for it is never advisable to allow the main branches of fan-trained plum trees to become too old. It is possible to use laterals as replacement shoots when necessary. Remember that plums not only bear their fruit on naturally-produced spurs, but also on young wood. Therefore much of the current year's growth should be retained each season.

Watch the trees throughout the summer; cut out and burn immediately any dead wood that appears. Look out also for suckers coming up from the roots, and cut them right back to their origins. It is not advisable to root prune plum trees, and neither plums nor damsons are summer pruned in the normal sense of the term.

Cherries

Before considering how and when to prune cherries, I must explain that there are two main types – the sweet cherry, which is usually grown as a standard tree, and which takes years to come into cropping, and the sour or cooking cherry, which is usually grown as a fan-trained tree on a shady north wall but can be cultivated as a bush. Few people grow sweet cherries in their gardens because they take up too much room as standards, and they are self sterile – they need the pollen of another suitable variety flowering at the same time to make their blossoms set. (For suitable pairs of varieties, i.e. the kind that act as 'mates' to one another, read another book of mine, *The Compost Fruit Grower.*)

If standard cherry trees are going to be planted in grass they need to be 40ft apart. Buy three-year-old trees and aim in the first five years to produce a good strong framework of branches. This means that the leaders (one-year-old end growths) on each branch must be cut back by about half late in every winter for five years. Some gardeners prefer to leave every other leader at full length after the second year of planting. They claim that fewer branches are broken this way, and annual cropping is assured. (Sweet cherries are notorious for seeming to want to crop only every other year.)

Of course, during the first five years after planting, rubbing branches may need to be shortened, and growths may be removed that tend to spring up perpendicularly. After this early period, however, little or no pruning needs to be done other than removing the dead and diseased wood and cutting out crossing and rubbing branches. Do this if possible in August or early September.

Fan-trained trees

Because a standard cherry tree takes up so much room, many people prefer to have sweet cherries growing as fan-shaped trees. The method of training is similar to that of plums. Aim to have the branches 10in. apart from one another. As these are being formed, you will discover during the summer numerous little growths being produced all the way up their length. Remove unwanted ones with your thunb and fore-finger – the idea is to leave laterals spaced out evenly at 4-in. intervals. By doing this the fruiting spurs on the branches will not be too crowded. The laterals which are left spaced out at 4in. apart are pruned back early in July to within 5in. of their base. As soon as all the leaves have fallen, these same laterals are pruned back further still – that is to say, within two buds of their base.

The one-year-old leader growths at the ends of the branches are shortened back by half early each March for the first five years after planting. After that they can be left alone. The sweet cherry varieties will produce plenty of fruiting spurs naturally but, ten years after planting, these spurs may be found rather long; they can be reduced by half early in March with the idea of reducing the amount of blossom produced and so concen-trate the available elaborated sap into the remaining flowers.

Sour cherries

Generally speaking, the only sour cherry grown in the garden is the Morello. For the first four years treat the bush tree similarly to the sweet cherry. From the fifth year onwards, however, the pruning changes, and in the winter cut out whole branches here and there to thin out the long, whippy wood on which the fruit is borne. Every year the tree produces masses of this type of wood, and every year it must be thinned out. After ten years it will probably be necessary to cut out about half the wood each season. The result of this severe pruning will, of course, be that more fruit-bearing wood will be produced for the following season.

Unfortunately, the Morello cherry frequently suffers from a serious disease known as brown rot. This may kill numbers of young shoots every year. To prevent the trouble from spreading, watch the bushes carefully each spring. If you notice any branches failing to leaf, cut them out immediately and burn them. It's always best to do this before the tree comes into flower.

Fan-trained cherries

When a fan-shaped Morello cherry has been trained against a wall or fence for eight years or more, there is always a tremendous amount of old wood to be cut out each winter and an equal quantity of long lengths of new wood which have grown in its place. The gardener has to cut out whole branches that were tied carefully to the wires the winter before. The aim is to tie in the new wood evenly all over the tree – a lot of work will be involved here.

The ideal thing is to have a strong shoot developing from the base of every young branch that is bearing that season. Cut out the long whippy shoot which has just borne the fruit, and tie in its place the long length of young wood that has been made that season. Thus every winter, when the wood that has cropped has been cut out, new shoots of a similar length will be available to tie in their place.

It is best to buy three-year-old Morello cherries which have already been grown in a fan shape by the nurseryman. These, however, are not cheap, and it is possible to plant one-year-old specimens called maidens and then early in March prune them back to within about 8 or 9 in. of soil level, to just above a bud. As a result of this hard pruning hopefully three strong growths will develop, the top one of which is tied perpendicularly to the wires and the other two trained out at an angle of 25 degrees.

The following winter the upright growing leader should be cut back hard to within about 6 or 7 in. of its base, while the other two branches are cut to within 8 in. of their base. During the summer, the shoots which develop as the result of this hard pruning should be watched carefully. In the case of the main leader, only three shoots should be allowed to develop, one upright and one on either side, making three shoots in all. The side ones are trained out to an angle of 25 degrees.

On the two lower branches the summer growths should be thinned out to leave one trained at an angle of 45 degrees and the other trained along the wire almost parallel to the ground. Similar pruning is done the third season and as a result a perfect fan should be produced. Once the branches do radiate out there should be little difficulty in cutting out some of the old wood each winter and tying in the young wood to take its place.

Although the methods advised are ideal, a modified form of pruning has been adopted by many gardeners who are short of time. The fan tree is planted and all the laterals and leaders cut back by half during the first five years. At the end of this period, the tree should have produced plenty of wood which is tied in a regular fan shape. From then on new wood is allowed to grow just as it will, and each winter three-year-old branches are cut out and some of the young wood tied in in its place. The rest of the young wood is just cut hard back.

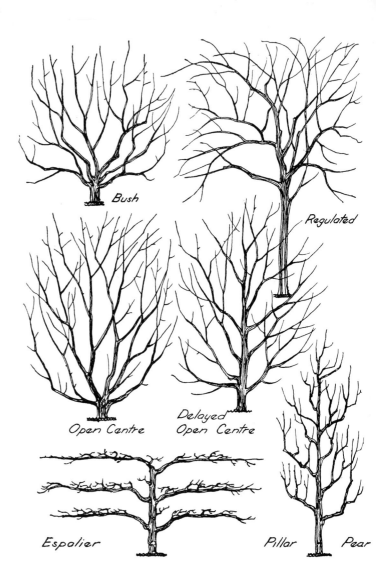

Bush

Regulated

Open Centre

Delayed
Open Centre

Espalier

Pillar   Pear

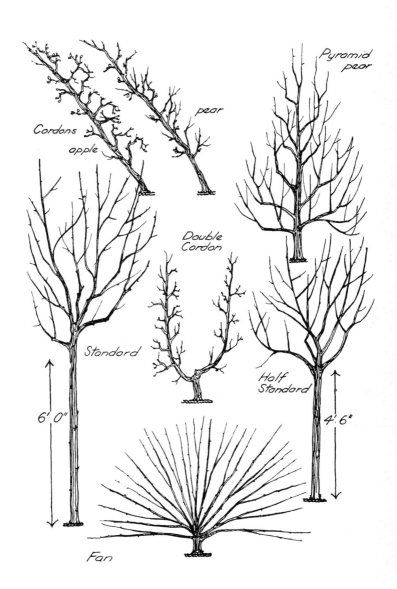

Cordons apple

pear

Pyramid pear

Double Cordon

Standard

Half Standard

6' 0"

4' 6"

Fan

7 Apple trees

There are so many systems of apple pruning that this chapter will necessarily be a long one. Some experts say that it's better to throw away the pruning knife and let the tree grow naturally, while others advise regular, rather severe pruning because they say that you get better, cleaner, larger and more colourful fruits which naturally give greater pleasure and satisfaction. Some methods lie in between the two. For ease of picking, spraying and general management, pillar trees have been adopted with great success. I have therefore divided the chapter into the following sections:

1. Forming and pruning a bush
2. Spur pruning.
3. The regulated or thinning system
4. Forming and producing a standard or half-standard
5. The delayed open centre tree
6. The pillar system
7. Dealing with a young tree

Cordon apples are dealt with separately, in Chapter 9.

Forming and pruning a bush

The normal bush apple is described as open centred. That is to say it is goblet-shaped. A tree two or three years of age trained in this way can be bought from the nurseryman ready for planting. On the other hand, it is cheaper to plant a single-stemmed one-year-old maiden. This normally consists of one long straight shoot. If there are a number of side shoots growing out from the side of the maiden then the nurseryman calls it a feathered maiden.

Plant the maiden in November, and start to form the bush by cutting it back to a height of $2\frac{1}{2}$ ft above soil level at a point just above a bud. If the maiden is feathered, prune back a little any side shoots growing below this cut. The idea is that the leaves on these side shoots will manufacture plant foods during the following spring and summer: thus the roots will be fed, and finally better top growth will result.

Because the maiden tree is cut back hard, three good strong growths should develop and these will form the basis of the future branches. If more than three shoots result, the weakest ones should be cut back to within 1 in. of their base to just above a bud. The three strong growths, which should be evenly distributed along the top of the young tree, should be pruned back about half to just above an outward pointing bud. When doing this, always aim to leave the tops of the young branches level. If any side growths are developing down the main stem, cut them back within an inch of their base; the following year cut them out altogether, right the way down to their base, leaving a clean stem.

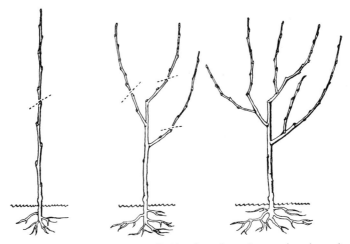

Maiden or one-year-old tree (left). Second year's pruning (centre). Third year's pruning (right)

As the result of pruning the three leaders, each one should produce two more, and so at the end of the second year there should be at least six branches instead of three. These should be evenly spaced around the central stem on which they are growing. They, in their turn, will be pruned back by half, and once again the number of branches will be doubled. Because the tops of these young branches have been kept level by pruning, they should all be roughly of the same strength and length at the end of the third year.

At the end of the third year the laterals are not pruned back – this enables them to form fruit buds. The only ones cut back are those that tend to rub other shoots or that appear diseased.

The main framework of the tree has now been formed and the gardener can now decide whether to adopt the thinning system or the spur system.

Spur pruning

The spur system was invariably adopted by our great-grandfathers, who said that every branch should be a cordon. It was devised in the days when labour was cheap and apples were commonly grown in the vegetable garden. The system was a simple one; it consisted of cutting back the one-year-old laterals each winter to within 1 in. of their base. At the same time the one-year-old end leaders were normally cut back by half, or, in cases where they were growing very strongly, by only a quarter.

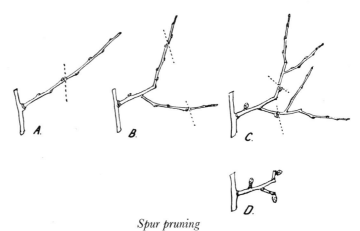

Spur pruning

A. The lateral   B. The same lateral after pruning   C. After second year's pruning   D. The formed spur

Pruning of the laterals hard back usually resulted in two further laterals being produced at that point, and probably a flower bud (usually called a fruit bud) lower down. The following season both these laterals were cut back hard, and gradually what were called fruit spurs were produced, each one bearing a number of fruit buds together with a number of laterals. After a time there could easily be 300 one-year-old laterals produced up a single branch, and each lateral had to be pruned back hard in the winter. So year after year the work increased. Sometimes, because of starvation or because the tree was grafted on to weak stock, laterals ceased to be produced and quite long spurs were then covered with fruit buds.

When the spurs were long and carried more than six or seven fruit buds, the plan was to prune so as to reduce the length of the spur by half.

I have purposely written all this in the past tense because spur pruning is seldom advised today, let alone carried out. However, readers who have taken over a garden containing spurred trees may like to continue to follow the plan detailed above. If trees make too much growth under this system, either because they are naturally strong varieties or because the tree is growing on a very strong stock, then it is necessary to root prune. Root pruning in itself is an expensive operation and so is seldom done today, though in Victorian and Edwardian days it was a regular operation.

The regulated or thinning system

Most people use this system today because (a) it entails a minimum of work, and (b) the trees come into cropping far more quickly. After all, the thinning system is almost nature's own plan and trees crop far earlier when unpruned! The young trees must be pruned quite hard for, say, the first three years if a maiden is planted. Exactly the same plan is advised for forming and pruning a bush tree. After the third or fourth year the tree is left almost alone: the leaders are not cut back, and the laterals are left at full length. However, a certain amount of thinning-out does take place: for instance, diseased wood is removed, and branches that tend to grow into one another are cut back. Prune the rubbing branch back to a lateral further down. Try to make the branches evenly spaced, and see that the centre of the tree is not cluttered up with wood which prevents light and air getting in to ripen the fruit buds.

The is the kind of common-sense pruning which I like to demonstrate. It's really letting an apple tree grow as it wants to grow, with just a certain amount of thinning out. The resulting tree is not so 'standardized' as the spur-pruned tree, and perhaps not so neat, but it is a most effective minimum-work fruit producer.

The disadvantage of not pruning trees at all is that they tend to produce small fruit, and diseases like scab which mark the skins are more difficult to control. It is much easier to spray a tree properly when the centre is open and the branches are well spaced out.

Forming and producing a standard or half-standard

The bush apple will purposely be grafted or budded on to a weak or fairly weak stock so that it will produce a small or moderately-sized tree that will crop early. The standard or half-standard tree must, however, be grafted on to a strong stock so that it can produce a good length of stem and strong branches above. Standard and half-standard trees are usually bought as three-year-olds, the initial work of training having been done in the nursery. Half-standards are usually on stems $4\frac{1}{2}$ ft tall, and full standards on stems 6ft tall. These trees are seldom planted in gardens today because they eventually take up too much room and the fruit is difficult to pick. Standards are most suitable for planting in grass, and half-standards are good for planting in poultry runs.

Readers who want to train their own standard trees from maidens should plant the one-year-olds where the trees are to grow but should not cut back the main leader. Any side growths on a feathered maiden will be cut back in June to within four leaves of their base with a pair of secateurs, and if secondary growths result on these laterals, these must be pruned back to within one leaf of their base by mid-August.

Because the maiden is not pruned, it should reach the desired height the following winter, and then, if it is to form a half-standard, a cut is made just above a bud at $4\frac{1}{2}$ ft from soil level. If it is to form a full standard, make a cut just above a bud at 6 ft from soil level and if for any reason the stems should not have grown to this height by the end of the second year, leave the maiden alone until the third winter before 'topping' it by pruning.

As a result of stopping or pruning back the main upward growing shoot, branches develop at the desired height in the same way as on bush trees. These branches are pruned for the next three years as described for bush specimens, but eventually a good framework of branches will have been formed. Thus you have a bush tree on a tall stem instead of on a stem 2 or $2\frac{1}{2}$ ft from soil level. After the third or fourth year the thinning system should be adopted because the branches are too high up from the ground for anyone these days to want to adopt a regular spurring plant.

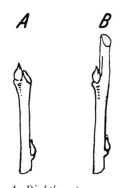

A. *Rightly cut*
B. *Wrongly cut*

The delayed open centre tree

The delayed open centre system of pruning is more complicated to describe than any of the other methods here. Generally speaking, the aim is to allow the centre leader to grow upwards and not to attempt to produce a goblet- or cup-shaped tree at all. By adopting this method, however, bigger trees are produced in a shorter period of time than under the bush system, and yet, on big trees, young growth is more easily distributed and earlier crops result.

Aim to develop branches from the centre stem which grow out almost parallel to soil level. These are sometimes called flat branches. It has been discovered that blossom buds form quicker on branches grown in this way. If, at the same time, these branches can be spaced out right up the length of the centre stem so that they are not one exactly above another, then the fruit will get the light and air it needs and will colour and ripen well. Aim to have a branch on one side of the tree corresponding to a branch on the other side of the tree: do this by making a notch or nick just above a bud on the maiden, as shown in the drawing on p. 70.

If a v-shaped nick is made with a sharp knife just above a bud, then that bud produces a lateral or side growth. If on the other hand a similar nick is made just below a bud in the one-year-old wood, then a flower or fruit bud will be formed.

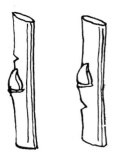

The notch above the bud makes it develop into a growth bud but the notch below makes it develop into a fruit bud.

You can use this knowledge to produce side growths or branches where you want them. Where you don't want either a lateral or a fruit bud to be produced, carefully cut out the bud altogether.

Because it is necessary to ensure that the centre growth grows perpendicularly in the case of a delayed open centre tree (in future this will be abbreviated to a DOC tree), when the main shoot is pruned back to just above a bud the bud below this is cut out altogether. This ensures that the top bud grows upwards without any competition from a growth just below. Eight inches lower down, buds will be notched above, a pair on one side and a pair on the other. The desired horizontal branches will thus be produced opposite one another without being exactly above one another. The following year the same scheme is followed. The main leader is pruned back by about a quarter to just above a bud, the bud below this is cut out, and then notches are made in the bud lower down so that pairs of branches can be produced. This work continues until the trees are about 8 ft in height. It should be possible to produce trees of this height in the first five or six years. During the whole time, the pruner will be trying to get the correct buds in the tree. Thus if a shoot has to be shortened on one side of the tree, the corresponding shoot must be shortened on the other side of the tree.

If any strong laterals are produced which are not needed as branches they must be cut out completely, that is to say right down to their base. If a pruned lateral is to be prevented from making further growth, then the end bud must be nicked just below its base, as shown in the drawing. There is, however, no cutting back of the laterals in the normal way, as in spur pruning, because the main supply of blossom invariably occurs on these side shoots. No shoot or branch, however, must be allowed to shade the one below very much, and if this is seen to be happening at the end of five or six years, one of the branches must be removed altogether.

At the end of the eighth year the tree will be formed, and it is then that the centre is cut out at, say, 7 ft. From then on it is important not to allow any of the branches to become static or stagnant. Branches must be regularly furnished with young wood about 9 in. to 1 ft long. Although it is true to say that the majority of the laterals must be left to form fruit buds, some may have to be pruned back to encourage the production of more laterals.

After some time the lower branches may tend to droop to soil level; they should be pruned to a point where a lateral grows upwards. If it is thought that the tree is growing too tall, then you can cut back the main growth to a side branch growing out lower down. In cases where gardeners have weak-growing varieties budded or grafted on to weak-growing stocks, it may be necessary to prune back the side branches fairly hard when the trees are well established or they may not make sufficient lateral growth.

The pillar system

This is really a commercial system. The principle of it is to plant 750 trees to the acre in rows 12 ft apart, with the trees 5 ft apart in the rows. The trees are budded or grafted on the Malling II or Malling Merton 104 stocks, and once they have reached their pre-determined height, say 10 ft, they never alter in shape or size. The pillar tree consists of an upright central stem from which radiate various types of lateral growths. There are no side branches at all in that sense of the word. The idea is to form an upright permanent support for the heavy crop of fruit that is going to be produced on the lateral growths.

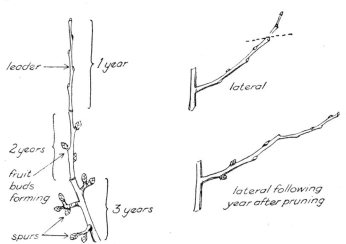

These growths fall into three age groups. The one-year-old lateral that has grown during the past season is not pruned. The result is that fruit buds are formed freely along almost its entire length. The following winter it is, therefore, pruned by cutting back any one-year-old growth that has remained at its tip. This means that this lateral, though two years of age, is back to its original length. It should now produce good fruit.

The following winter, of course, this lateral will be three years old and it must now be cut hard back. The pruning is, in fact, done right back at the point from which the lateral grew out from the main stem, or at least to within $\frac{1}{8}$ in. of that point. The result of this hard cutting back to the three-year-old lateral is that a new lateral will be produced the following season, and thus what is called a 'pillar pruning cycle' commences all over again.

Thus the mature pillar tree consists of a strong upright stem bearing three-year-old laterals which have just fruited, two-year-old laterals which are to crop the following season, and one-year-old laterals which are to form fruit buds the following season. To summarize:

1. Leave unpruned a large number of one-year-old laterals
2. Cut off the terminal growths at the tip of the two-year-old laterals
3. Cut back the three-year-old laterals to within $\frac{1}{2}$ in. of their base. (Leave two laterals for each foot of height of the tree.)

Dealing with a young tree

If a one-year-old tree is planted, it is cut hard back to within 30 in. of ground level and any side growths present are cut back to within $1\frac{1}{2}$ in. of the main stem. During the second winter, the leading shoot is cut by half to just above a bud and the first lateral or side growth below the leading shoot is cut back to within $\frac{1}{2}$ in. of the main stem. All the other laterals are treated in the same way, with the exception of one which is left unpruned. This should be a moderate length. During the third winter, carry out exactly the same type of pruning, but instead of leaving one lateral below the leading shoot unpruned, leave two; however the first lateral immediately below the leader must not be one of these two. Of the growths made below the present year's growth, two one-year-old laterals can be left unpruned.

Thus it can be said that in subsequent years it is possible to leave two one-year-old laterals unpruned for each annual tier of growth, while below this annual tier six one-year-old laterals may be left. When the leading shoot has reached a height of 10 or 12 ft it is cut back and all side growths made from then on are treated as described for the mature trees.

8 Various ways of pruning pears

Some people think that if you know how to prune apples you know how to prune pears, but this isn't quite true. Pears on the whole produce fruit spurs more quickly and easily than do apples, and there are perhaps more differences in varieties. You have to be sure that you know the spreading or drooping varieties like Beurre d'Amanlis and the very upright-growing varieties like Doyenne du Comice. The spreading varieties naturally need encouraging to grow upwards, and varieties that grow like church spires need pruning to keep them open. However the general instructions given in Chapter 7 do apply to pears, and especially so perhaps in connection with the spur system, because pears are seldom grown on the regulated or thinning system. I never advise growing pears as standard or half-standard trees, since these tall trees never seem to produce such good quality fruit. Pear growing, therefore, should be concentrated on bush trees, cordons, or the pillar system.

When fruit spurs get too long, reduce their length as shown here

As far as normal bush trees are concerned, for the first five years prune back the one-year-old end growths of the branches by about half, and cut back the one-year-old side growths by about three-quarters. After eight or nine years it should be possible to prune back the leaders much less, and most gardeners from that period onwards will only cut back a quarter of each leader. This maintains reasonable vigour in the tree.

Follow the general pruning system as described for apples to produce a goblet-shaped bush tree on a stem about $2\frac{1}{2}$ft high. Then, because pears produce their fruit buds in abundance, it won't be long before the spurs are overloaded with these buds. It is far better to have, say, 500 good strong flowers than 5,000 weak ones, so it pays to thin out the fruit spurs after the first eight or nine years to reduce the number of flower blossoms, as well as to allow the tree to grow moderately vigorously. The longer spurs can be cut back with a pair of secateurs to an obvious fruit bud lower down, while the spurs that have tended to spread out can be thinned as shown in the drawing.

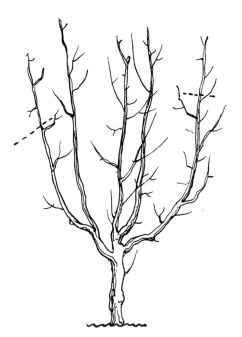

Cut all these branches back by a quarter of their length

You can thin out the spurs winter after winter if necessary. Of course, if the tree stops growing after, say, ten years – and some varieties of pears are apt to behave like this – you will need to cut back the branches themselves by about a quarter with the idea of forcing the tree into producing a strong leader. Having done this, the new branches can be trained on year by year by cutting the leader back by a quarter each season. This will maintain the tree's vigour.

Summer pruning

Pears react very well indeed to summer pruning and especially to the anglicized Lorette method, details of which are in Chapter 13. Hard summer pruning proves particularly useful in varieties that naturally make a lot of woody growth and so don't come into cropping early. Two that fall very definitely into this category are Pitmaston Duchess and Beurre Hardy.

Growing pears as pyramids

In many gardens pears are grown successfully as pyramids, or cone-shaped trees as they are sometimes called. In some ways the system is similar to the delayed open centre system already described. The idea is to allow one branch to grow right up the centre of the tree: growing out from this are evenly spaced out branches, the lower ones of which are longer than the upper ones – hence the term pyramid.

The way to prune this kind of tree is to allow the main one-year-old leader shoot to be shortened to within 15 in. of its base each year. The cut is made just above a bud, and the two buds below this are removed carefully with the sharp blade of a knife. This encourages the main leader to grow upwards without any local competition and, at the same time, it should force buds lower down to form side branches. As I explained earlier, the way to ensure that a bud does grow out to form a strong lateral is to make a little nick above the bud: this forces it into growth.

These side growths are pruned back to within 9 in. of their base to just above a bud, and once again the two buds below are cut out carefully. Any laterals, by the way, not required to form branches are cut off right the way down to their base to prevent them growing further. Those laterals that are pruned back, of course, form branches, and sub-branches may develop on these. The aim is to produce lower branches of a greater length than those on the upper reaches of the tree, for this makes not only pruning easier but also spraying and picking.

By careful pruning, the tree produced will look like the one in the drawing on page 63, but when the tree has filled its allotted space and reached the required height leader pruning can be reduced to the minimum. It may only be necessary, for instance, to cut 1 in. off each leader. This not only keeps the tree sufficiently vigorous, but also, interestingly enough, helps to encourage root activity. By the time the tree is nine or ten years old you will probably need to thin out the spurs as shown in the drawing on page 73, and there may be some suckers coming up from the roots which you will have to prune right down to their base.

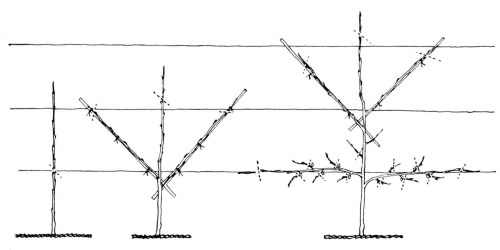

The method of training espalier pears. Year 1 (left), Year 2 (centre), Year 3 (right)

Espaliers, dual and triple cordons

Pears lend themselves to being trained in unusual ways such as espaliers and dual and triple cordons. Many of course are grown as cordons at an angle of 45 degrees and this method of culture is dealt with in detail in Chapter 9. In Chapter 12 the espalier system is described, which can be used for apples as well as pears.

In the case of dual and triple cordons, cut back the maiden when planted by about half to just above a bud. Two strong growths are then encouraged, one on either side of the stem, and any other laterals that develop are cut out carefully when they are 1 in. long. So at the end of the first year after pruning back, two strong laterals should be available which are trained to form a large v. Then push into the ground two strong bamboos, up which the two branches will be trained. They should be 18 in. apart. Gradually the laterals can be bent to form a u and here, of course, is where the bamboos come in to hold these growths in the right position. At the end of the second year, in December, the two leaders are cut back by about half, the growing laterals at the top are trained on, while the side growths are pruned back hard to within about three buds at their base.

When it's necessary to form a triple cordon, the maiden is cut back equally hard but three growths are allowed to develop, one vertically and the other two as laterals. The centre shoot invariably shows more vigour than the other two so its end must be pinched back when 15 in. long to let the two side shoots catch up in vigour. The training is done with strong bamboos as before, and leader pruning and lateral pruning should be done in the same way as for the dual cordons. Remember that it is always possible to ensure that the right buds grow out by making a v nick in the bark just above each one.

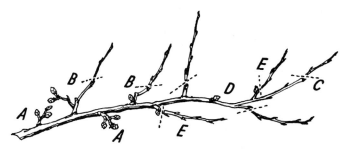

A. *Spur with no lateral* B. *Lateral plus spur*
C. *Pruning leader* D. *Fruit bud*
E. *Pruning back to fruit bud*

Special notes on varieties
Some varieties, like Jargonelle and Josephine de Malines, bear on tips and these cannot be spur pruned in the ordinary way. Prune these varieties in the early years to shape and form the branches and then grow them on the regulated system. Varieties like Beurre Diel and Doyenne d'Eté generally need fairly hard pruning throughout their lives, while varieties like Conference, Doyenne du Comice, Durondeau, Hessel, Marguerite Marillat and Beurre Hardy can generally speaking be pruned lighter than most varieties.

9 Cordon apples and pears

A cordon apple or pear is really a single-stemmed tree which is normally trained at an angle of 45 degrees. The stem is tied with wires and the laterals that grow out from the side of the stem are cut back quite hard to produce fruiting spurs right the way up its length. Cordons can be grown in both a vertical and a horizontal position. In vertical cordons there's no check in the flow of sap as there is when the stem is bent, and so fruit spurs are not formed so easily. In horizontal cordons the trees grow so close to the ground that you have to bend right down to prune, spray and pick the fruit.

Because the cordon grower wants his trees to crop early, with a minimum of unnecessary growth, he will choose the stronger-growing varieties grafted on to the MG stock and the weaker varieties on type M2 stock. In the case of pears the most suitable stocks are either Quince c or Quince a. When bought on these stocks, the trees must be planted shallowly because if the union of variety and stock (known as the scion) is buried in the soil the variety itself may send out roots and ruin the beneficial effect of the root stock on which it was grafted.

For a double cordon, the trees are usually planted 5 ft apart in the row, with the rows themselves 6 ft apart. To form these cordons the one-year-old maiden is cut back to just above a bud 12 in. from ground level, and during the following summer the two top shoots that grow are trained out carefully, one to the right and the other to the left. The shoots are tied to bamboos. Once the laterals have reached a length of 8 in. the leading growth must be bent round into a perpendicular position and then tied to a bamboo to make it grow vertically.

At the end of the first year there should be two leading shoots forming a U, and in December these two shoots should be cut back by about a third each to just above a bud. The leaders are then allowed to grow unrestrictedly upwards throughout the summer and any side growths which develop can be cut back by half. The following December the leading

A fine cordon apple

79

growths are then cut back by a third and all the side shoots are pruned back to within 1 in. of their base. In this way the double cordon is formed.

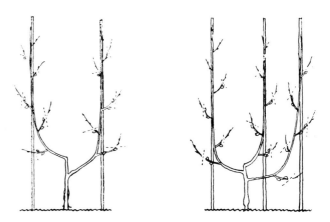

Double and triple cordon

For a triple cordon, the one-year-old maiden tree is planted early in November. This is cut back to within 12 in. of its base the following February, at a point just above a bud. Hopefully three growths will now develop: the one at the top will be trained upwards vertically, while the two lower ones will be trained out parallel with the ground for the first 8 in. as described for the double cordon. After 8 in. these two side growths are trained perpendicularly up bamboos so that by the end of the year there should be three growths running parallel to one another. These three growths must be cut back absolutely level the following December. It is usually necessary to reduce them by half. This should ensure that the three leaders from the three main growths will grow equally strongly. Subsequent training and pruning is just as for double cordons.

Single stem cordons are usually planted 2 ft apart and trained up wires stretched tightly in between posts as shown in the drawing. Sometimes the trees are planted upright to start with, and then six months or a year later trained at an angle of 45 degrees. Bending them sideways at this time is meant to ensure a check in the flow of sap and as a consequence the earlier production of fruiting spurs. Another advantage of training cordons at an angle is that a greater length of stem is possible within the given height. In fact when a cordon has got to the top of the wire or fence provided, it can be untied and re-tied at a shallower angle.

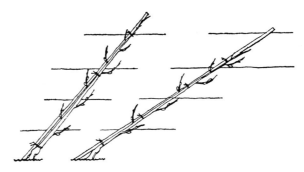

An oblique cordon cut down as it grows longer

Single cordon pruning

Plant the maiden as early in November as possible. The following February cut it back by half to just above a bud pointing in the right direction. This hard cutting back should not only ensure the production of a strong extension shoot but should also stimulate a number of laterals into growth. In some years one or two fruit buds may be introduced. The laterals can either be pruned back in the summer on the anglicized Lorette pruning method, or can be pruned back in the winter in the normal way within two or three buds of their base. The following December the extension shoot or leader will then be cut back by about half. The laterals which develop as a result will either be summer pruned or will be cut back to within two or three buds of their base in the winter.

I have known some professional gardeners who have been against pruning back the extension shoots at all. They claim that if these remain uncut the cordons come into bearing much more quickly. There is always the danger, however, of a great deal of bare wood up the stem if the leader is not pruned, and with a cordon it is most unprofitable to have great lengths of stem that are not producing any fruit at all.

It is possible to encourage dormant buds to break out on bare lengths of stem by what is called 'knife edge ringing'. The bark should be cut right round the stem with a sharp knife just below the last bud to break above the bare patch. When the cordon has reached its allotted space it should be untied, as I have already explained, and tied in again at a lower level. But even after this, if the cordon reaches the top of the wire or fence, cut the cordon back to some lower lateral which is growing upwards. This lateral can then be pruned back by about half and gradually once again the cordon will start extending its length. In this way the vigour of the cordon will be maintaned and this is a great advantage.

The normal method of pruning once the cordon is established is to cut back those laterals that are 1 ft long or so to within two or three buds of their base. If there are any very strong shoots, say 18 in. or 2 ft long, it is better to cut these out with the sharp blade of a knife right to their base with the idea of preventing them growing again. When the spurs have got too long or there are too many fruit buds, a certain amount of

A heavy cropping cordon pear

spur thinning is necessary. This means that some of the fruit buds are cut out altogether and the length of the spur is thus reduced. A cordon tree always tends to produce far more blossoms than are necessary and this spur thinning helps make the flowers stronger and more likely to set properly. It is far better to spur thin in the winter than to spend hours thinning blossom in the summer. The aim should be to have fruit spurs spaced out about 9 in. apart over the length of the cordon.

Every winter, of course, you will need to remove the dead and diseased wood and, if big cuts have to be made, clean them up with the sharp blade of a knife and paint them over with thick white lead paint. Don't let diseased wood lie on the ground – pick up any pieces and burn them. Use a little paraffin if necessary to make sure that it is properly burnt up.

Summer pruning
There is no type of tree on which the anglicized Lorette type of pruning works better. I call it anglicized because I have had to modify this French method of pruning to suit the wetter British climate. The method is described fully in Chapter 12.

10 Apricots, peaches and nectarines

Apricots, peaches and nectarines are mostly grown as fan-shaped trees against walls. Under these conditions they tend to be pruned in a similar manner. Apricots, on the whole, produce their fruit spurs more naturally and more profusely than peaches and nectarines, and most of the fruit is produced on short spurs. Some varieties, it is true, produce good blossom on young wood but this does not set as easily as the blossoms on a spur. With all three fruits a certain amount of summer thinning out and pinching back is necessary.

Apricots

Because apricots are subject to bacterial dieback, and peaches and nectarines to gumnosis and leaf curl, there's a lot to be said for doing as much of the pruning as possible in the summer. The idea is to leave in position the young shoots that will actually be needed for replacement or extension, but to remove any surplus shoots. It's more pleasant to prune in the summer than in the winter, and the spores of the silver leaf disease are not about then. On the other hand, because apricots have the unfortunate habit of losing whole branches from dieback, it is always advisable to retain one or two young growths with the idea of having them available to replace dead branches at any time.

Late varieties of apricots should be grown against fences or walls facing south, but a south-east wall will do for earlier varieties. In the colder parts of Britain I wouldn't advise trying to grow apricots at all. Most gardeners will purchase a fan-shaped tree three or four years old. The two early varieties are Large Early Montgamet and New Large Early (Rivers) which can be picked in July, and the two late varieties are Hemserk and Moor Park which can be picked in August.

Training a young tree
If you want to train your own tree right from the start buy a maiden from a reliable nurseryman. Plant it in early November in properly prepared soil, and cut it back to within 5 in. of soil level the following February or early March. This hard

pruning should make two strong growths develop, one on one side of the single stemmed tree and one on the other. Any other laterals growing out from the side of this maiden should be carefully rubbed out when they are about ½in. long. The tree can then concentrate on growing the two laterals and they should grow strongly in consequence.

These strong laterals (which should be trained to form a wide v by tying them to strong bamboos pushed into the ground) should be cut back hard during the following winter – say to within eight buds of their base. Make the cuts at an angle of 45 degrees just above an outward growing bud. As a result of pruning the laterals in this way four good laterals should grow out as seen in the drawing on page 86, and each of these will be pruned back by half in the winter just above a bud once again. Any shoots in excess of the four desired should be removed the moment they start to develop, that is to say when they are ½in. long.

Of course, as a result of pruning the four growths back hard, eight strongish growths should be produced the following year together with a number of laterals. This time most of the laterals will be kept and tied up to wires fixed to the wall or fence, running parallel to one another about 2ft apart. The leaders must be cut back by a quarter in the winter, and by that time a nice fan-trained specimen apricot tree should have been formed with all the branches about 18in. apart, one from another.

In the fifth year, if all has gone well and there isn't any serious frost, the tree should produce a nice crop. From this time onwards little pruning needs to be done in the winter, for it is better on the whole to leave the leaders and any suitable laterals so that they can be tied into the wires in the summer. Some of them can take the place of any diseased or dead branches that have to be removed.

Every spring the gardener should look over his fan-trained apricot trees as they start to grow, and if any shoots are tending to grow out perpendicularly from the wall they should be pinched out with the thumb and forefinger right the way back to their base.

In late June or early July, a certain amount of summer pruning may be done on the laterals that have filled their allotted space. Some of them have been tied in carefully to a vacant spot and by early July they may have developed too well. Take a sharp pair of secateurs and prune this growth

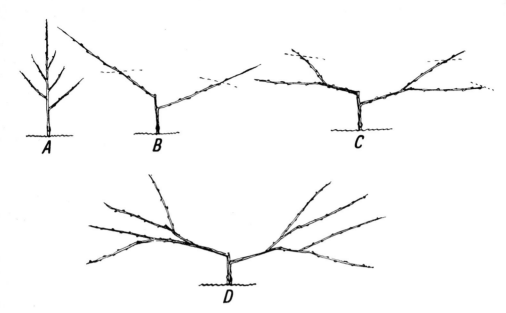

Forming a fan peach. A. The young tree as planted. B. The result of hard pruning the first year. C. The result of the second year's pruning. D. The tree starting to take shape

back to just above a bud to keep it in check. If, at the same time, unwanted one-year-old side growths are noticed, cut them back to their base.

Look at the fan-trained tree again in October before all the leaves fall, and if any branch is obviously unhappy – if the leaves are drooping or are bright yellow in colour – then it may be advisable to cut out the branch altogether before the trouble spreads. Thick branches may have to be sawn off: the wound should be cleaned up afterwards with a sharp knife and painted over with white lead paint to which paste dryers have been added – they help the paint to dry quickly and prevent the spores entering.

Peaches

Fan-trained trees

The early varieties of peaches can be grown as bush trees and their pruning is described later. The later varieties must be grown against a wall or fence, preferably south-facing.

Peaches can be bought fan-trained from the nurseryman. If you want them on a 3ft stem or leg to give them height before they fan out, you will have to pay a little more. If you want to train your own fan peaches, buy maidens and prune and train them in the same way as for apricots. At the end of the fourth year, however, more disbudding is necessary than in the case of apricots. Remember that the fruit is borne largely on the one-year-old wood that hasn't grown too strongly. Each growth that has fruited, needs to be pruned right back each season (after the fruit has been picked) to a young lateral growing as near to it as possible. Disbud by pressing the shoots with the thumbnail alongside, when they are about 1 in. long: they will come away from the wood on which they are growing easily and freely. Disbudding is best done in two periods, the second time ten days after the first. If it is all done at once it gives the tree too much of a check.

Look at the drawing on this page and you will see that the plan is to leave a lateral (marked A) growing right at the base of the fruiting shoot. The second shoot (B) is left about half way up, and the third or extension shoot (C) will be found

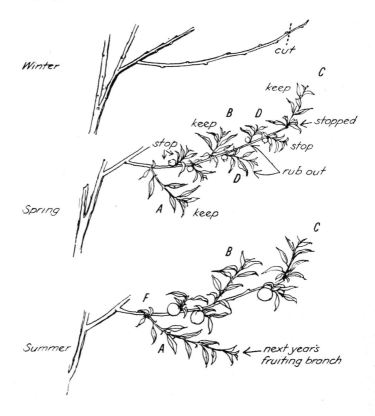

right at the end of the growth. The idea is that growth A will be retained because it will produce the flower buds (followed, of course, by the fruit) the next year. Growth B is retained to produce leaves in which elaborated sap will be manufactured to feed the swelling peaches. Growth C is called the 'sap-drawer' and its function is to pull the sap upwards as the weeks proceed.

In the middle of July growths B and C are usually cut back about half way down with secateurs. Summer pruning is especially necessary in a wet year. Growth A is not touched at all unless, for some reason or another, what are called sub-laterals grow out. If they do appear they must be pinched right out in July with the thumb and forefinger (D in the drawing).

In the winter, the branch that has fruited will be cut back as F and in its place will be tied the new young lateral A, now really a branch. It helps, by the way, if during the summer lateral A is tied down to the wires; this will prevent it growing away perpendicularly from the wall or fence. By tying it in almost parallel to the fruiting branch on which it is borne it will be much easier to tie it in securely in late autumn or early winter.

Some gardeners do not advise autumn or winter pruning until early March. They say that only then can blossom buds easily be distinguished from wood buds. There seems, however, to be very little point in this, for the great thing is to retain young ripened wood which has been specially selected for this in the early summer, and then to try and make certain that it is spaced 9–12 in. apart all over the wall. It is always better, by the way, to rely on moderately strong growths and to remove the exceptionally strong laterals altogether.

Bush trees

It has been said that gardeners who can prune blackcurrants can prune bush peaches, and there is a lot of truth in this. Good growth must be encouraged each season to ensure a heavy crop of fruit. Once the trees are four or five years old you will need to cut out a certain amount of wood each year to encourage new wood to develop. The trees must be properly fed – proper pruning is bound up with proper manuring. Early every May, get hold of some really well-rotted compost or sedge peat and apply four or five large forkfuls to each bush tree for a spread of about 4 or 5 ft. In addition, apply a fish manure with a 6 per cent potash content at 5 oz to the square yard all round the trees as far as the branches spread.

Buy bush trees two or three years old. Plant them early in November, shallowly but firmly. Before mulching in May prune all the branches back by half. The idea is to cut back the one-year-old leaders to just above a strong side shoot lower down growing in the right direction. You will only need to do this if the leaders are no longer than 1 ft: if they are about 2 ft long there is usually no need to prune at all that year.

Each May prune in a similar manner, that is to say cut back the leaders and any dead branches. Continue this kind of pruning for the first six years and after this cut away some of the main side branches, too, so that the sun can get right into the centre of the bush to help ripen and colour the fruit. By thinning out the branches as necessary each year the peaches can be picked more easily. There are always some branches which insist on crossing right into the centre of the tree, and they will have to be pruned back quite hard. Cut them back hard to their base, making a clean smooth cut, and then, to prevent any trouble, coat the wounds with thick white lead paint.

Every May from the sixth year onwards some of the lower branches will need cutting back and some of the crossing and rubbing branches must be removed. Try and remove three or four branches each season to stimulate growth. Don't worry about producing a beautifully shaped bush. Remember the peach pruner's rule, 'If in doubt, don't.' Make sure you have plenty of growth each season, and therefore if a tree is not growing well prune it quite hard one year – you will be surprised at the way the bush springs into vigorous growth the following season.

Nectarines

Nectarines are pruned in exactly the same way as peaches. They are grown almost entirely as fan-trained trees with the exception perhaps of Early Rivers, which are ready for picking at the end of July, or John Rivers, which can often be picked in mid-July. The main difference between the true nectarine and the peach is that the nectarine needs more frequent watering when the fruit is swelling, especially in dry years. If insufficient water is given at this time the nectarines tend to split.

11 Various ways of pruning vines

The 1960s and 1970s have seen a resurgence of vine growing out of doors in Britain, particularly in the southern counties. There are three main methods of pruning vines, the first two of which can be carried out both under glass and in the open, while the third is more suited to open air culture or at least open air culture with some tall cloche coverage.

The first method is sometimes called the long rod system but more frequently the spur system or spurring. The idea is to cut back quite hard the laterals which eventually form spurs on which the fruiting wood is produced. This system was very popular about 100 years ago. The second method is called the extension system, the idea being to allow one vine to occupy as large a space as possible. The laterals are trained out evenly over the wall or fence and are tied to wires. Very often the extension system and the spur system are combined, so that once the branches cover a large area the laterals can be cut back hard in winter. Some summer pruning may also be done in addition.

In the greenhouse

The spur system

Buy a good three-year-old rod about 8 or 9ft long. The vine should be pot-grown and when it arrives the ball of soil should be carefully broken up and roots spread out well before planting them shallowly and firmly in November. Prune back the rod to within 3ft of its base early the following January. The spring and summer after planting, let the main rod grow as long as it wishes. Any side growths that develop on this rod must be cut back to within 2ft of their base: the leaves on these laterals will manufacture elaborated sap which will help to extend the roots. Laterals stopped in this way must be pruned back to within one bud of their base in the winter.

It is at this time of year – November or December – that the main growth (which perhaps by now has reached the top of the greenhouse) is cut back to within about 6ft of its base, to just above a bud. This will encourage not only a new extension shoot to develop, but also the production of laterals

90

right the way down the stem. These side shoots are stopped at about six leaves in the summer, and they are pruned back to within one bud of their base in the winter. The extension growth is stopped at the top of the house in the summer and is cut back by about half in the winter.

Once a strong rod has been produced, pruning each season is fairly simple. In the first place, rub out in the spring any growth that may develop at the top of the rod because you don't want any extension growth shoots at all. Then examine the young laterals that have grown out as the result of pruning back hard in the winter, and leave the most vigorous one on each spur. It is on these selected laterals that the fruit will be borne. The growths should be stopped at two joints beyond the bunch of fruit or at one joint if there isn't any space for

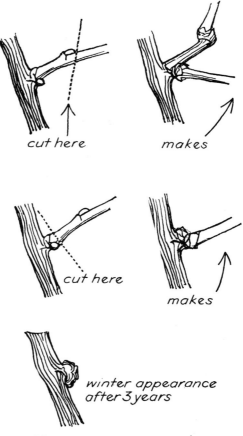

cut here   makes

cut here

makes

winter appearance
after 3 years

The correct way to prune grapevines

later extensions. At the same time cut off the tendrils with a sharp knife. Any secondary shoots which grow out as a result should be pinched back immediately just above the first leaf, and this must be done again and again as the shoots regrow throughout the season. If any laterals are not bearing fruit cut them back with sharp secateurs just above the sixth leaf. These laterals can then be tied into the wires – as can the laterals that are bearing fruit.

The long rod system

In the long rod system, the idea is not to prune back all the laterals as advised with the spur system but to allow some of them to grow to full length or almost to full length, and so let them fruit. Gardeners who have adopted this system say that better fruit is borne on these rods than with the spur system. It is always difficult, however, to know which rods to retain and which rods to cut out. Personally, I never recommend the long rod method of pruning vines because it usually results in a lot of useless wood being produced.

Out of doors

The spur system

Some varieties grow quite well out of doors. They include Chasselas Vibert, Royal Muscadine, Tokay Frontignan and Miller's Burgundy. Two-year-old planting canes may be bought with rods about 6 or 7ft long. They should come expots early in November and should be planted carefully the moment they arrive, i.e. once the roots have been unravelled. After planting firmly in a suitable position cut the young rod back hard to within 1ft of its base to just above a bud. If the vine is to be grown on the spur system it must from then on be treated exactly as advised for greenhouse-growing.

The horizontally trained system

The alternative is to grow the rods on what is called the horizontally trained system. The rod is planted in November and then cut hard back to within 18in. of soil level about the middle of January. All the shoots that develop as a result are retained – they are trained out fan-shaped on wires for the first twelve months. This helps to build up a really good root system.

The following November, the bottom two laterals are cut back to within 3ft of their base and they are horizontally trained on to the wires, one on either side of the main stem.

The central shoot is tied upright and shortened back to within 4 ft of soil level, cutting just above a bud. Any growths in excess of these three are pruned back to within one bud of their base.

During the following summer laterals will, of course, break out from the horizontal shoots and those which develop on the lower side of the stems are rubbed out with thumb and forefinger when they are about 1 in. long. On the upper side of the stems any laterals closer than 1 ft are removed at the same time. The side growths which develop on the central stem are retained every 18 in. or 2 ft with the intention of using them to train the vine horizontally along the wires the following winter. It is best if these stems can be nearly opposite one another to achieve the right balance.

The horizontal stems chosen for the extension of the vine are shortened back in the winter to 3 ft, as before. The central or extension growth, of course, is trained vertically upwards to form a continuance of the main stem. The laterals produced on the horizontal branches the following year are cut back to one bud in the winter, and, directly a horizontal branch has covered its allotted space, the terminal shoot is rubbed off each summer. It is fairly simple to retain this attractive shape by the usual cordon method of pruning.

During the summer it will be necessary to thin – not more than one lateral should be allowed to grow out from the spur. This pinching out should be done very early in the life of the lateral. The laterals on the lower side of the branches must also be rubbed out, and the moment that bunches of grapes are seen on the laterals these should be stopped at two leaves beyond. If no fruit develops, summer pruning should be done to the fourth leaf, counting up from the base of the young laterals.

The extension system

Instead of growing the vines on the cordon system or the horizontal system, you can use the extension system. This means that you don't confine the vine to one stem and when you carry out the first pruning back of the young rod you train out in a fan shape all the growths that develop, and cut these back in their turn to within about 3 ft of their base the following winter. Then select, say, three growths on each rod, one at the apex of the growth to act as an extension shoot and to train upwards and outwards, and two strong laterals, one on either side of the rod, which you may train out to help produce the fan shape.

The system undoubtedly ensures the production of good roots and tends to impart vigour and energy to the vine. Once enough young rods have been produced to cover the space desired, pruning back in the summer should be carried out as with the spur system, and laterals can be cut back to within one bud of their base in the winter. It always seems to me that this method of culture is most consistent with the natural growing habits of the vine, and certainly in the past I have seen tremendous crops on one plant. For instance, a vine growing on the extension system can actually cover such a large wall space that if the length of all the rods was added up it would come to at least a quarter of a mile. Such a well-grown specimen can produce over 800 bunches of grapes, each about 2 lb in weight. The problem, of course, with British vines is the weather. Given lovely sunshine all through the summer and into September, you will be able to grow good grapes out of doors.

The Guyot system

The Guyot system can be used with no difficulty to grow vines out of doors in the open. If you live in a cold area, cover your vines with tall T cloches.

The drawings demonstrate far more clearly than words exactly what happens. Note the pruning points – they are marked quite clearly – and note also the growths which develop as a result of pruning. At the end of the third year, the main two branches which are retained should be 5 ft long. They must be this long if they are to be vigorous enough to bear the following season. Please note in Fig. 4 how one of the shoots has been cut back to two buds and the other to ten buds. The long shoot is the one that will be allowed to crop and the growth that has been pruned back to two buds will provide the necessary replacement for the following year.

Now in Fig. 5 you will notice quite clearly that the replacement is growing; it is tied up to the galvanized rod provided and is pruned back when it gets to the top. The laterals on the other shoot are pruned back to just above the second leaf, which in its turn is just above each bunch of grapes. This summer pruning should be done just as these bunches come into flower, because experiments have shown that it assists in the setting of the blossom.

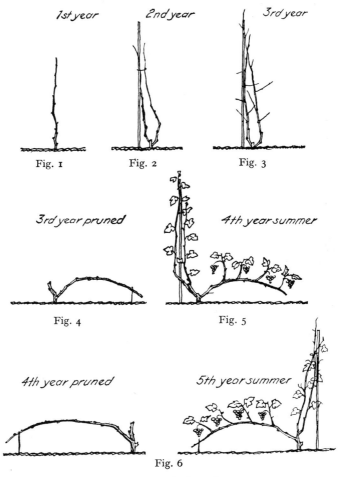

Guyot method of pruning

Note what happens in Fig. 6 because this is the work that must be done each subsequent year. All the fruiting wood is cut away; one of last year's shoots is pruned back hard to within two buds of its base and the other shoot is trained in a curved fashion before being pruned back a little – by about eight or nine buds. From this time onwards, year after year, one of the two shoots which has been trained up the rod is retained and the other one is curved as shown in the drawing. About eight bunches of fruit will be borne on each rod of the vine and this means that it is possible to have between 6 and 10 lb of grapes each year. The rod to bear the grapes should never be longer than 3 ft 6 in. and most gardeners in fact prefer to have it at 3 ft.

Guyot summer pruning

If the vines are growing under tall T cloches or access frames, from the middle of June onwards you must open up the side panels to let in more air. It always pays to 'top' – that is to prune back by about 4 or 5 in. – the shoots bearing the bunches of grapes. This should be done just as they come into flower, to help set the flowers. If any side shoots develop as a result of the topping, let them reach 4 in. and then snap them off at their base rather as you dis-shoot tomatoes. The other side-shoots which have developed before the topping can be shortened back to within three buds of their base. Vines only need to be dis-shooted when they are growing under tall T cloches, because the mass of foliage under the glass must be reduced.

When the vines are growing in the open and are not covered with cloches it is necessary in the summer to shorten back to within one leaf of their base all the new shoots which grow out from every leaf axil. When the replacement shoots reach the tops of their stakes, they should be topped at that point and the resulting new shoots should be pruned back to within two leaves of their base. Rather more leaf can be allowed in the Guyot method when the vines are in the open than when they are under cloches. In late September the leaves actually shading the bunches of grapes can be cut off with secateurs.

12 Summer pruning

Few people want to go out into the garden on an icy cold day to prune fruit trees. Others, understandably, are equally reluctant to prune when it's pouring with rain. Of course it isn't always raining, snowing or icy cold during the winter months but somehow it always seems to be one of these three on the day you have set aside to do the work. For this reason summer pruning has become increasingly popular, especially the type of summer pruning which obviates the need to prune in winter. The laterals are pruned in summer and the leaders in spring.

There are two main types of summer pruning. The first may be described as the normal English method and the second as the Lorette system. Professor Lorette was an expert who carried out a large number of trials in the south of France and wrote a book on the subject. His scheme must be modified somewhat to suit conditions in Britain, with its higher rainfall. I have therefore coined the term 'anglicized Lorette' pruning, and I have been able to demonstrate that the system works very well indeed in all but the wettest parts of Britain, especially on cordons, bush trees, espaliers and pyramids.

The gardener summer prunes to encourage the formation of fruit buds. He also uses this method to check and direct the growth of the tree. In addition he is thinking about improving colour and appearance – particularly in the case of dessert apples – as a result of the increased amount of light and air that can reach every part of the tree.

Ordinary Summer Pruning
The idea here is to prune back the laterals – please note never the leaders or one-year-old extension growths – and to do this some time during the summer. Most gardeners agree that it is better to do the work a few weeks before the particular variety concerned is to be picked, the idea being that if the laterals and leaves are removed then the sunshine will be able to get at the apples and give then a nice rosy colour. This means that, with early varieties like Worcester Pearmain and

English summer pruning

Fortune, summer pruning can be carried out in August, whereas with varieties that are picked in September or October, the majority of the summer pruning can be carried out during the second week of that month.

It is always a mistake to summer prune too early, because secondary growths tend to develop. This is particularly true in a wettish year. Summer prune a lateral in July, and by the end of August it will have started growing again; a tremendous amount of sap will be wasted as a result. The idea should be to summer prune so that there will be no secondary growth at all. It is sufficient to reduce the lateral by half or to cut it back, if it is fairly weak, to within, say, eight buds of its base. With the varieties that tend to produce their fruit buds on the tips of laterals, summer pruning may be inadvisable. I wouldn't summer prune an Irish Peach for instance, or a Cornish Gilliflower – or even a Worcester Pearmain except when it was perhaps fifteen years old and had settled down into fruiting on the normal spurs. Some gardeners believe that it is better not to cut the laterals back with a sharp knife or with secateurs, but to break them off with the back of the knife blade (brutting).

In the past professional gardeners have tended to summer prune in this way all espaliers, cordons and other 'shaped' trees, whether it was really needed or not. The operation was regarded as necessary from the point of view of tidiness. No thinking gardener would do this today. Laterals which need pruning in the late summer to let in light and air must be carefully reduced, and sometimes it is better to cut out a lateral altogether, if it is in a place where it isn't needed, than just to prune it back by half.

The anglicized Lorette system

I started to take an interest in anglicized Lorette pruning when I was sent a little booklet on it, many years ago. It seemed to make sense, and what appealed to me was the fact that it was possible to do all the pruning in the summer and no pruning with icy fingers in the winter. I tried out the system on my own cordons, and found it worked admirably both in Cheshire and in Kent. I have since used it on wall trees with 'grid-irons' and with pyramids, and in fact wherever this method of pruning has been recommended it has worked well.

With old-fashioned English summer pruning the gardener aims to get his fruit to ripen better, but the Lorette pruner is after the production of fruit buds. After all, most people have to grow their trees in a garden with limited space. We are often forced to grow trees in some unnatural way, and yet we want to ensure that they bear heavy crops. Nobody wants a tree with barren branches and, in fact I always think that if a specimen is not productive it is just space-wasting and should be used for firewood.

Don't think it is wrong to prune trees in the summer – in fact with plums and other stone fruits it is always better to cut out branches during the summer months when the silver leaf disease can't give trouble. Therefore you could say that any type of pruning is best done in the summer and I often saw quite large branches out of apple trees during July and August. The old wives' tale about excessive bleeding is in general quite untrue. Don't be frightened of pruning in the summer months – in fact all wounds heal much better in summer than in winter.

The only reason perhaps that many gardeners insist on pruning in the winter rather than in the summer is that they are so busy during June, July and August doing other jobs in the garden, whereas there is much less to do in December and January. This anglicized Lorette method does, however, ensure that the work is spread over a 12- or 13-week period, the idea being to prune the laterals to within an $\frac{1}{8}$ in. of their base with secateurs when they have reached a stage of semi-maturity. This usually means when they are 6 or 7 in. long, and the earliest and the strongest laterals usually reach this stage by the middle of June. Please note that the pruning has to be done as hard as this, and note the words 'to within $\frac{1}{8}$ in. of their base'.

On the other hand, you only prune the laterals that have reached the 7in. length and you leave the shorter ones until later on. Every fortnight or so from the middle of June until the end of September, go over the trees, and on each occasion prune back the laterals that have reached the right length. If you find two laterals growing out from almost the same spot during one of your fortnightly visits, cut one of these back quite hard and leave the other until the next visit. No shoot, as I have said, should ever be cut back until it is ready, and any laterals that do not reach the right length by the end of September are left until the following summer. All this sounds very revolutionary, but it really does work.

What I have said concerns laterals only. Do not touch the leaders at all in the summer. Leave them until the following May and then prune them according to their length and strength. A leader that is, shall we say, 18in. long, might be cut back by about 8in.; but a leader on the other hand only 10in. long might be reduced to about 4in. The idea is to ensure that the buds at the base of the leaders break out so that there will be further laterals to prune back hard and so more fruit buds will be formed.

The anglicized Lorette pruner wants to encourage the development of the stipulary buds which are hidden in the bark around the bases of the laterals. Pruning back each lateral hard to within $\frac{1}{8}$ in. of its base forces these dormant buds into growth. Sometimes further laterals are produced but generally fruit buds are produced prolifically, and if the little stubs of the laterals are examined the following October, many will be found to have fruit buds. Fortunately, as the trees get older the proportion of fruit buds to further laterals definitely increases.

13 Pruning trees to special shapes

Fruit trees can be trained into all kinds of unusual shapes. The French are very fond of doing this, as are the Italians. I have seen wonderful specimens at the School of Horticulture at Versailles and at the Horticultural College at Florence – trees trained into huge cups or mugs, triangles, and many other shapes.

L'Acure system

To train trees under the l'Acure system buy maiden one-year-old trees about 4ft tall. Plant them 3ft apart, and if more than one row is needed the next should be 5ft away. The trees must be trained on posts and wires: drive 6-ft posts firmly into the ground at either end of the rows and stretch wires tightly between them, the first wire 18in. from the ground, the second 18in. higher up, and so on.

Six months after planting, when the roots have had a chance of settling down and growth is commencing, the maidens should be bent over to form a half moon, the tip being attached to the wire with a short length of tarred string. During the early summer, a number of laterals should arise from this curved length of stem and all of them except one

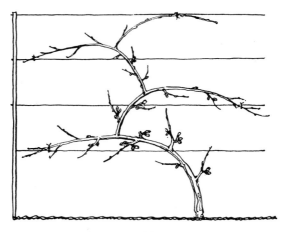

right in the centre should be cut back with a pair of secateurs to within ⅛in. from the point at which they start. This should be done when they are 6 or 7in. long.

The chosen lateral should be allowed to grow to its heart's content because it is eventually going to be bent over in the opposite direction to the original one to form another half circle. It is not usually possible to do this until the following summer when it is about 3 or 4ft long. This process of arching the growths first one way and then the other, as shown in the drawing, continues year after year, one main lateral being chosen for the purpose each season. Each year the other laterals are summer pruned back to within two buds of their base in June or early July, and if any other laterals develop in August or September these are pruned back in the same way. Follow, in fact, the anglicized Lorette pruning method for these laterals.

No other pruning is necessary, either to the leaders or to any of the laterals – in fact, the leaders are not pruned because as the tips are curving downwards they don't make any further growth. The result of this arching and the Lorette summer pruning is that fruit buds are developed quickly and the trees settle down into cropping almost immediately. I have known pears grown on the l'Acure system produce a useful quantity of fruit in their first season and, as the years progress, the crops have got heavier and heavier.

Almost all varieties grow well under this system providing the necessary pollinators are present. Doyenne du Comice, that rather difficult pear, grows well under the l'Acure system when the variety Glou Morceau is planted nearby.

The palmate system
The palmate tree is trained on the cordon system. Choose a well-grown maiden with a young lateral growth on one side. The main shoot is then trained to the right and the lateral growth to the left so that they both run parallel to the ground. Keep these branches parallel to the ground and tie them to wires about 18in. or 2ft from the soil level. If you like, you can have a second layer of branches, and in this case a lateral is allowed to grow upwards and is pruned back the following winter by about half. The two best laterals that develop are then trained one on one side and one on the other. It should be possible to tie these two down to horizontal lines towards the middle of September so that by the winter there will be two

sets of horizontal branches growing parallel to one another. A lot of the work can be done in the summer by completely removing unnecessary growths and so allowing the tree to concentrate on the two laterals which are to be kept. These palmate-trained trees look best planted around the edge of a border: they take up little room and form an attractive and useful surround.

Espalier trees

Espalier trees are usually formed by the nurseryman but some people like to try and produce their own specimens on what is called the horizontal training method. Start with an apple, say, on the Type M7 stock, or a pear on the Quince A stock. Choose a one-year-old tree with a nice clean stem 5 ft long, and having, in November, planted it out in the place where it is to grow, cut it back in February to within 12 in. of soil level, to just above a bud. As a result, three strong shoots should be produced from the three top buds: the middle one is allowed to grow upwards and the other two are trained out at an angle of 45 degrees so that they balance one another, one on either side of the main shoot.

The following winter prune back the main upright growth by about half, once again to just above a bud. At the same time the two side growths should be bent down so as to run along the wire which runs parallel to soil level. These two growths should now be shortened back by about half. It sometimes happens that the side growths are not strong enough the first winter to pull down, and in that case they are just lowered a little. The following winter they will be lowered once more to the horizontal position.

Now the idea is to take one leader at the end of the upright growing shoot and once more to select two laterals which can be trained first at an angle of 45 degrees and then lowered the following season to form the second tier. Strong wires are again provided, to which these branches are tied.

Year after year, this general method is followed so that you can get branches growing parallel to one another to form the espalier tree. It helps, of course, if the laterals on these side branches are pinched back in the summer when they are showing three leaves, so that when the trees are properly established the anglicized Lorette method of pruning can be carried out each summer.

14 Root pruning and ringing

Though root pruning and ringing are completely different operations they are designed to have the same effect. When a tree is happy and growing vigorously it has no desire to reproduce its own species. It is only when it fears that it is going to die that it tries hard to reproduce its own species quickly. A young tree, for instance, just grows and grows and has no desire to fruit. It is only as it gets older that it crops.

We sometimes find a tree branch which is attacked by canker at the base. This one branch will crop heavily while the others make nothing but growth. Root pruning is designed to take the flow of elaborated sap down to the leaves. An attack of canker, therefore, has a similar effect to ringing.

Cropping, then, is bound up with the right balance between the mineral sap which comes up from the roots each season and the elaborated sap which is manufactured within the leaves and which can be passed down to the soil so as to make new roots, or which can go to the spurs to help produce fruit and/or make new fruit buds. This scheme is dealt with in greater detail under the heading of ringing.

Root pruning

Root pruning was adopted by Victorian gardeners long before people knew anything about root stocks and their effect. If a gardener found that a pear or apple tree was making far too much growth or was taking up too much room, he dug the tree up and cut off the deep-striking roots with the idea of encouraging more fibrous roots. Root pruning is not practised much today because of the amount of work it involves.

Some people say that it is very good for trees up to six years old, but in fact it should not be necessary to root prune specimens as young as this. Readers who want a small tree should buy one guaranteed grafted, in the case of apples, on the Type ix stock, and in the case of pears on the Quince c stock. As a result you get earlier fruiting without needing any root pruning.

If root pruning has to be carried out, the effect, of course,

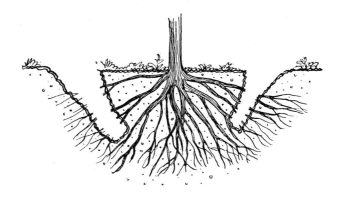

is to cut off much of the water and minerals which are being pumped into the tree, and thus the exuberant growth is checked. This check may only last two or three years, but during the period the tree will have started to crop and by this very fact will not be able to grow as strongly. Heavy cropping always drains the vitality of a tree and so excessive growth is just not possible.

Carry out root pruning late in the autumn just after the leaves have fallen. When trees are of a manageable size the whole root system may be lifted out of the ground and the coarsest shoots shortened to half their length. Never cut away the fibrous roots, just the thick anchorage roots. Don't make jagged cuts, but see that they are clean and smooth, and try and make the cut point downwards to encourage the fibrous roots to grow upwards. Immediately after root pruning the tree should be replanted in the same spot. The soil should be firmed thoroughly and the trunk should be tied to a good stake so that the tree cannot be blown about during the winter.

With bigger and older trees, root pruning must be done by the half circle method. Dig out a trench 2 ft wide and up to 4 ft deep, 3 ft away from the trunk of the tree, on one side only. Cut off all the roots found during this excavation. The following year another half circle is dug around the other half of the tree, the same distance away and the same depth, and once again all the thick roots are sawn off. Complete root pruning, therefore, takes two years.

Don't be under the misapprehension that an apple or pear tree has one tap root and that if this is cut off all will be well. This idea that fruit trees have tap roots is a fallacy – they have deep-striking anchorage roots but not just one tap root. So don't waste your time planting a tree on a flat stone or concrete slab to prevent the tap root from developing. The anchorage roots will in fact merely grow to the edge of the concrete slab and then strike down below.

Ringing

The operation known as ringing or bark ringing has now largely taken the place of root pruning. To explain the principle underlying the ringing process let me say that the leaves are the manufacturing centre of the tree and that the roots send up the minerals or what may be called the raw materials to be 'made up'. These raw materials are carried in the water in the wood vessels on their way to the foliage while the manufactured plant food (elaborated sap) is circulated throughout the tree, as I have already suggested, to assist in the growing processes or for storage purposes in the roots. It flows through the bast cells which are just under the bark.

Therefore, when ringing, the flow of crude sap upwards to the parts above the ring is not interfered with, but the manufactured plant foods cannot pass downwards below the ring, either entirely or partially depending on how severely the ringing has been done. Bark ringing, therefore, may completely shut off the food supply to the roots or do so only partially, and as a result there will be a corresponding concentration of elaborated sap in the branches of the tree above the ring.

Bark ringing does not take long to do. It is best to do it in the spring when the tree is in full blossom. It works very well with apples and pears, and can also be done on plums and cherries though here there is a little danger of gumming. Ringing does encourage the formation of fruit buds and the setting of the flowers which are produced. Though the fruit picked from a rung tree is usually more highly coloured, it unfortunately tends not to keep too well.

The operation consists of removing a ring of bark about $\frac{1}{4}$ in. wide right the way down to the wood and a few inches below the level of the lowest branch. With bush trees the work has to be done, as a rule, just above soil level, but with standard trees it can be carried out at a height of 4 ft from the ground. Work with the sharp blade of a knife and cover over the wound afterwards with adhesive tape or thick white lead paint to which paste driers have been added.

Some people prefer what is known as the two half-ring method and in this case two half-rings of bark, one 4 in. above the other, are removed at opposite sides of the trunk from one another. If the tree is old, say 20 years of age, then the rings may be $\frac{1}{2}$ in. wide, or even $\frac{3}{4}$ in. wide in the case of a strong growing variety like Bramley's Seedling or Newton Wonder. In the case of very vigorous trees on very strong soil and with strong stocks, the rings may be allowed to overlap somewhat. Until the tree has settled down keep these half-rings open every season at blossoming time. This may be necessary for about three years.

Never carry out ringing or even root pruning for that matter unless the trees are growing very strongly and are not fruiting. Ringing old trees that are not growing, or stunted trees, is very risky indeed.

15 Useful hints

There are a number of hints and tips on pruning that have been impossible to include in the previous chapters. The following methods enable a fruit grower to increase the weight of the crop and to ensure that the trees fruit regularly.

Shoot circling
Sometimes it is necessary to encourage the formation of fruit buds in other ways than pruning. One of the best methods is shoot circling. The laterals, instead of being pruned back hard, either in the summer or winter, are left at full length and are then bent round in a circle in November or December. The work may take some time and the trees will look most peculiar afterwards but the result is that fruit buds are produced on the curl and it isn't difficult to cut back the laterals to one or more of these prominent fruit buds in the winter.

Trees that respond to this treatment particularly well are

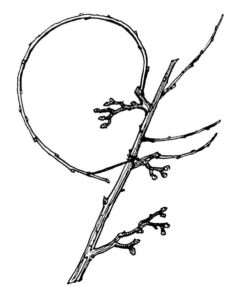

Shoot circling

Laxton's Exquisite, Laxton's Superb and Ellison's Orange. I have known a leader or end growth treated in this way to prevent further growth taking place at the end of a branch. A check occurs, and fruit buds may be produced; even if there is another growth it will only be a short one.

Branches at the top of a wall

When trees are grown as espaliers, in the long run the branches, or certainly the young wood on the branches, will inevitably grow over the top of the wall and look untidy. Thin out the laterals thus produced, to leave only one or two per spur; having left these at their full length the whole of the summer, they will develop fruit buds lower down and it will be possible the following winter to cut back to just above a prominent fruit bud and so prevent any further growth at that point.

Spur thinning

When a tree has been grown for years on the spur system (in particular), a whole series of longish spurs covered with fruit buds appears all the way up the branches. These fruit buds are rather an embarrassment to the grower – each one may produce a dozen blossoms and the result is that, at flowering time, the tree has to cope with trying to feed literally millions of blossoms, with the result that none of them is particularly strong. It does pay, therefore, to reduce the long spurs by less than half or to cut out every other spur completely. Generally speaking, a good gardener will do both. He will cut out, say, every other spur and reduce the remaining ones by about half. There is a danger, of course, of overdoing this work in one season, and it is probably better to let the operation take two years. It is most important not to cut back a spur unless you are sure that there's a really plump fruit bud lower down.

Sometimes spurs get long and lanky and the bulk of the fruit buds are produced at their tips. In this case, very little pruning back can be done and you will have to concentrate on spur thinning only. However the flowers set far better after spur pruning and the results well repay the effort.

Knife-edge ringing

Knife-edge ringing consists of making a cut through the bark right round a young shoot, and down to the wood. No actual bark is removed and the cut made soon heals over. There is, therefore, only a slight check in the downward movement of the elaborated sap and this means that the length of wood above the knife edge ringing has just a slight check and as a result tends to produce fruit buds rather than excessive wood.

Actually, the modern system is rather more knife-edge notching, and this can be done in two ways: (1) just below the bud to ensure that that particular bud plumps up into a fruit, and (2) just above a bud, to make certain that this bud grows out the following season into a lateral. It is sometimes very useful, in the case of trained trees, to ensure that a particular bud will break out and form a strong shoot. In both cases the operation consists of making a cut about $\frac{1}{8}$ in. deep through the bark into the wood at an angle of about 45 degrees and then making a similar cut below the first one, at a similar angle but in reverse; you can then remove a wedge-shaped piece of bark and wood. The work is only done on one-year-old wood.

Sawing off big limbs

Very often, when buying a new house, you inherit trees that have been neglected for a number of years, and it may be necessary to saw out some quite large limbs to let in light and air or because the branches are growing into one another; even worse, some trees may be overpowering or overcrowding others. Sawing out branches must be done carefully and properly.

In the first place, never leave any snags – short ends of the branches which can never grow again and which remain a perpetual open wound and an entry point for disease. A branch should always be sawn right the way back to its base (see drawing). To make certain that the branch doesn't fall down when the saw cut has been made, say, three-quarters of the way through, thus tearing the bark and causing a nasty wound, always make your first saw cut upwards for an inch or so from the underside of the branch. Then you can start sawing downwards, and there will be no accident.

Clean up the saw cut with a sharp knife and leave it absolutely smooth; then the cambium layer, which lies just underneath the bark will have no difficulty in growing out and forming a nice callous over the wound. You can see this starting to develop in B. Paint over this smooth wound with a thick white lead paint to which, if possible, you should add paste driers, so that it hardens very quickly.

A

B

It is never advisable to prune an old tree too much at one time. Therefore, if it does seem to be necessary to cut out, say, a large branch in the centre of the tree as well as three or four other branches around the outside, do not do more the first year than take out the middle branch. The next winter you can start reducing the number of other branches or maybe start pruning them.

Reheading and dehorning

Sometimes garden trees get too tall and become difficult to pick and to spray. I usually advise reheading, that is to say, sawing down the branches to a point lower down where there is a nice young branch to take on the growth. When reheading make the saw cuts at such an angle that the wound has no difficulty in healing and the branch to which the cut was made has no difficulty in taking on the sap and so helping to produce a well-shaped tree.

Dehorning is carried out on the branches that have bent down to the ground through heavy cropping. They must be sawn back to a suitable branch growing in an upward direction – sometimes this may just be a question of sawing back to a very strong lateral. There is usually a growth further back on the tree which is growing upright and it is just above such a branch that the cut must be made. In both these cases follow the general directions already given for sawing out large limbs.

16 Evergreen and flowering shrubs

As I have said in the case of fruit trees and bushes, it is better not to prune at all than to over-prune. With shrubs it is equally true. Pruning, in fact, is by no means essential. A large number of jobs which one can do on shrubs are worthwhile but not vital. With rhododendrons and azaleas, for instance, it is always good to remove the old flowers as the petals fall – in fact before they go to seed. Do this to lilacs too. In this way the shrubs are saved from the exhausting process of trying to bear unwanted seed.

It may be necessary to prune a shrub because it has got too large, or at any rate because it has grown too big for the spot in which it is growing at that particular time. The idea is to shorten the bulk of the branches back to just above some little branch growing lower down. This work is always better done just before the buds start to grow out in the spring, so that the bush has a full season in which to recover. There are, of course, exceptions to this rule, for instance in the case of shrubs which flower in March or April or even before. Here it is advisable to wait until blossoming is over before pruning.

Of course, any shrubs which flower on the wood produced that particular season (commonly known as the current season's growth) can always have their shoots pruned back in the winter or very early in the spring. It is usual to treat most buddleias in this way. Other shrubs that are generally pruned by this method are the tamarix pentandra, some of the hypericums, and at least two spireas (japonica and aitchisonii). Often, after pruning large specimens, numbers of young growths are produced and these may have to be thinned out in the summer because there are too many of them too close together.

With both shrubs and flowering trees, it is most important to know which species or varieties flower on the young wood and which bloom on the wood produced the previous year. The latter category should always be pruned as soon after flowering as possible; as a result plenty of new wood is produced and this gives the shrub enough time to form the future blossom buds. With shrubs that flower on the young wood, the pruning is usually done late in the dormant period, that is, just as growth is about to commence. If the work were done as soon as the blooms faded, the new growth would be made at once and this wouldn't be well-ripened and hardened enough to over-winter.

Some shrubs, of course, give of their best when they are cut down almost to ground level in the late winter or very early spring – spireas like Anthony Waterer, for instance, and hydrangea paniculata. Then there are the bushes like the cornus or dogwood which are grown largely for the beautifully coloured bark produced on the young wood. These bushes are cut back hard in the winter to make a regular mass of reddish growth which, when the leaves fall in the autumn, looks most attractive.

Some shrubs should not be pruned at all – the magnolia, for instance, hates being cut in any way. Other shrubs in this category include andromeda, aralia, the Judas tree, coton-easter, daphne, desfontainea fatsia, garrya, gaultheria, grevillea, hibiscus, kalmia, lithospermum, parrotia, pieris, ribes, skimmia, veronica and viburnum.

The two main classifications

All shrubs can be roughly divided into two groups: (a) those that flower from June onwards, and (b) those that flower in the spring or early summer. In the former case the blooms are obviously produced on the growth made during the current season and in the latter case flowering always takes place on the wood produced the previous year. Study the growth of all the shrubs in your garden, and classify them.

The second section is by far the larger and with the great majority of shrubs, therefore, it is only necessary to thin out the branches, to cut out the weak wood, to remove the worn out or diseased shoots and so on. In the former case, it is just a question of cutting back the growth in, say, early April to encourage the production of shoots or branches which will flower in the summer. Do this, for instance, to common garden roses.

Notes on the pruning of some common shrubs

Abutilon   Shorten the branches if necessary the moment the flowers have faded. Look over the bushes after a very severe winter.

Arbutus   No regular pruning is needed, but in April it may be cut back if the shrub becomes too large, though severe pruning is not advisable.

Artemesia   Cut out some old wood each February. At the same time cut back the growths made the previous year, aiming to keep each bush as compact as possible.

Azalea   Cut off the flower heads the moment they have faded. If the bushes get too large you can cut out one or two branches quite low down in April, to encourage the production of new wood.

Berberis   When grown as a bush, thin out after the flowers have faded or cut back the longer shoots to laterals developing lower down. When grown as a hedge, always prune immediately after flowering and not a second time.

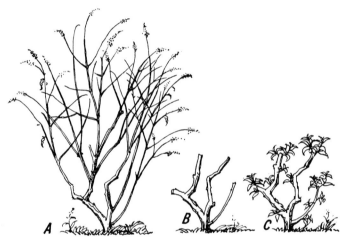

Buddleia A. Late autumn B. Pruning in spring C. Sprouting next spring

Buddleia   There are three main types.

 b. variabilis or *davidii*: must be cut back hard each year in February. In April thin out some of the young shoots.

 b. alternifolia: every year cut out some of the older branches almost to ground level in February. Thin out other wood if the bush appears crowded.

 b. globosa: immediately after flowering shorten some of the longest branches with the idea of keeping the specimen bushy.

Bay Tree   See *Laurus*.

Callicarpa   Thin out the branches when they get too thick; aim to keep as much young wood as possible. Cut back the leaders of the branches if they stick out too far over a path.

Calluna vulgaris   This type of heather is often called ling. Cut off the old flower heads the moment they fade. If the bushes get too overgrown it is better to replace them than to attempt to cut back too hard.

Ceanothus   This genus may be divided up into two definite groups (a) the spring flowerers which bloom on the growths produced the previous season, and (b) the summer- and autumn-flowering varieties which bloom on the growths which have developed during the year.

   (a) This group needs very little pruning to keep the bush in shape by light pruning immediately flowering is over.

   (b) Prune hard each February all the growth that has flowered the previous season. The stronger branches can be cut back to within 8 or 9 in. of their base and the very weak ones to within 1 in. of their base.

Ceratostigma   Thin out the little branches when they get too thick – cut off the flower heads the moment they fade. Very often branches are cut down by the frost but the shrub revives again in the spring.

Cercis (the Judas tree)   Over the first five years cut out a little wood here and there to keep the bush open. After that there should be no pruning to do other than removing dead wood.

Chimonanthus fragrans   Sometimes grown as a bush, and sometimes trained against a wall. In the former case, little or no pruning is necessary. In the latter case prune the moment flowering is over, cutting back the growths to within 1 in. of their base.

Choisya   Prune in April, cutting back the branches so as to reduce the size and keep the bush in a useful shape. If grown as a wall tree, prune hard the moment the flowers are over.

Cistus   Cut off the old flower heads the moment they have finished blooming. Thin out one or two branches if they are rather close together.

Clethera   Cut off the dead flower heads as soon as the blossoms fade. Thin out a branch here and there to let in light and air.

Colutea   Prune in February, shortening back the new growth to within 1 in. of its base. Some gardeners believe in no pruning, but then the bushes always grow long, leggy and large.

Cornus Let the shrubs grow for the first five or six years without any definite pruning. At the end of this period, if the shrubs appear overgrown, cut them back quite hard with sharp secateurs. Varieties which have lovely coloured barks may be cut down each year to within 6 in. of soil level, to produce plenty of strong colourful shoots in the winter months.

Cydonia Sometimes grown as a bush, sometimes as a hedge, and often against a wall. As a bush, don't prune. As a hedge, cut back quite hard the moment the flowers are over. As a wall tree, prune the young shoots to within 1 in. of their base the moment flowering is over.

Prune here after flowering

Cytisus

Cytisus The brooms are apt to get long and leggy if they are not pruned regularly. Cut the young growths the moment they have finished flowering to within 1 in. of their base.

Deutzia Prune the moment the flowers are over in the early summer. Cut away some of the old wood each season. Some gardeners prefer to prune more drastically only every three years. I prefer to do a little thinning out every year.

Diervilla Is sometimes listed in catalogues as *weigela*. There are two main methods of pruning a bush. The first is to cut back the branches that have flowered to within 1 in. of their base the moment the blooming is over, and the second is to adopt the thinning system advised for deutzia. I prefer the former method, but it tends to exhaust the trees and they don't last quite as long in consequence.

Erica These may be divided into two groups, the tall species and the dwarf types. In the latter case just cut off the old flower heads the moment blooming is over; in the former case, prune a little harder immediately after flowering, to prevent the individual specimens from growing too long and lanky.

Escallonia This can be grown against a wall or used as a hedge, or planted as a specimen. In the latter case, little or no pruning is necessary, but in the former cases, the plant must be cut back quite hard immediately flowering is over.

Euonymus japonicus When the bush is about five or six years old, one or two branches can be thinned out if they appear to be too thick. *Euonymus radicans* can be grown as a carpet beneath trees and in this case the plants should be cut back quite hard each mid-April.

Forsythia There are various species to consider.

> *F. euopaea, F. ovata* and *F. viridissima* should hardly be pruned at all.
>
> *F. intermedia:* prune back hard immediately after flowering, cutting out the old wood. Leave the fresh young shoots to flower next year.
>
> *F. suspensa* is excellent for a wall. Should be pruned the moment flowering is over. Cut back the secondary branches to within 1 in. of their base. As a result long growths are produced which bloom well next spring.

Fuchsia Can be grown as a bush or as a hedge. In the former case, cut back the youngest branches to within 1 in. of their base in the spring to keep the bushes compact, or if preferred leave well alone. In the case of hedges, prune early in the spring quite hard. In all cases examine the specimens in the spring and, if any branches have died from frost, cut them down almost to ground level.

Hamamaelis The second year after planting, cut back any branches that tend to cross and rub one another. Shape the plants in this way for five or six years and then there should be no need for further pruning.

Hydrangea   Most people grow the common hydrangea, *H. hortensis*, and its many varieties. These should be pruned after flowering, cutting out the old worn-out wood and encouraging the young to grow.

> *H. arborescens*, *H. radiata*, *H. cinerea* and *H. paniculata* (the deciduous group) are best pruned hard early in the spring with the object of removing the previous year's wood. Cut it down to within 2 in. of its base.

Hypericum   Commonly called St John's wort. In most cases it pays to cut back the growths that have flowered during the season at the end of the winter. It is convenient to cut them back by about half. Many gardeners prune *H. calycinum* and *H. moserianum* harder back still in the early spring. It is always possible to thin out the older wood in the spring, if the plants are getting too straggly.

Jasmine   Once again there are two main types.

> *J. officinalis* should be pruned after flowering by thinning out the branches here and there.

> *J. nudiflorum* should be pruned immediately after flowering, cutting out the growths to within 1 in. of their base. *J. primulinum* should be pruned in a similar manner.

Kerria   The moment the flowers are over, prune with the aim of removing the older wood and encouraging plenty of young shoots. Even after thinning out in this way, it is possible to shorten some of the past year's wood to keep the bush in bounds.

Laburnum   Thin out the branches here and there as necessary after flowering.

Laurus (bay tree)   Allow the tree to grow naturally for five or six years, and then cut back with secateurs any branches that spoil the shape of the bush. Pruning should be done in April.

Lavender   Always prune back quite hard either when flowering or immediately flowering is over. If a lavender hedge gets untidy it is possible to cut back quite hard about the middle of March.

Lonicera   There are various varieties, most of which need little pruning. What cutting has to be done should be carried out the moment flowering is over.

> *L. nitida* makes quite a good hedge and needs pruning three times during the summer.

Magnolia   Try not to prune magnolias growing in the open. If it becomes necessary from the point of view of shape, then

Spike just starting to grow.
When cutting the flowers later, cut the spike low

} last year's growth

Lavender

remove what branches that are necessary in August. When growing magnolias against walls, prune the *M. conspicua* types in May and the *M. grandiflora* group in April, remembering to tie in carefully all branches possible.

Mock orange   See *Philadelphus.*

Olearia   Once again there are two main types.

    O. haastii should be pruned immediately after flowering. Cut back the branches by about 3 or 4 in. If at any time the bushes get too long and lanky, harder pruning can be done about April.

    O. macrondonta is sometimes grown as a hedge and in this case it must be cut back hard with a pair of shears immediately flowering has ceased.

Philadelphus

Philadelphus   Often called the mock orange. Once again there
are two distinct types: the strong-growing group, and the
weaker-growing type composed largely of hybrids.

The strong growers, typified by *P. frandiflorus* and *P.
coronarius*, should be left alone except for a certain
amount of winter thinning, once every eight or nine
years.

The moment the flowers have died, prune the weak growers
to some point lower down where there is a nice strong
shoot growing. It is often possible to cut down almost
to ground level.

Pieris   Treat as for azaleas.

Pittosporum   Cut out a branch here and there in April just to
keep the bush to a nice shape.

Prunus   Some bush varieties, like *P. japonica* and *P. trioloba*, can be pruned by cutting the branches back to within 2 in. of their base immediately flowering is over. Other types are merely thinned as seems necessary.

Pyracantha   Some bushes are grown as specimens, and should be left alone. However most are trained against walls, and should be pruned on the spur system as advised for apples. Pruning is usually carried out in two stages, one early in the spring, and the second in the summer to cut back the secondary shoots.

Rhododendron   Cut off the flower heads immediately they fade. Cut back a branch or two in April when the bushes are, say, ten years old, to try and keep them in bounds. By removing a branch or so every two or three years, when the shrubs are overgrown, you can ensure some flowering and some growing shoots, which of course, will flower in a year or two's time.

Rhus   Prune in February to within 3 in. of soil level. When new growths appear in the spring, thin down to one per plant. Large leaves are produced like this. Wall specimens are usually cut back quite hard each spring. Bushes or small trees should only be pruned to shape. N.B. Some species can cause dermatitis and others are very poisonous – always wear gloves, and take great care.

Ribes (*flowering currant*)   No regular pruning is necessary, but you may need to cut out a branch here and there to keep the shrub in shape.

Romneya   Prune in February, cutting back the very thin shoots quite hard and reducing the longer growths by about 6 in. In April cut down any dead wood to ground level.

St John's wort   See *Hypericum*.

Salix   Most willows are grown for the beautiful yellowy-orange bark on the young wood. Cut hard each March, therefore, to within two buds of the base of the young shoots, and plenty more young shoots will be produced the following season, which will look beautiful in the autumn.

Spartium   Prune as for cytisus.

Spiraea   There are two main groups.

> The first group produces flowers on the end of the young wood, and as a result this has to be pruned back to within 2 in. of its base in February.

> The shrubs of the second group produce their blossoms on wood that has developed the previous year. The prun-

ing, therefore, is best done immediately after flowering with the idea of just thinning out here and there to keep the bushes within bounds.

Syringa (lilac)   Remove the flower heads directly blooming is over. Thin out the branches here and there in April, if necessary, cutting out the weaker shoots. Do this again early in June with the idea of concentrating the sap into the strongest growths. Any really old and straggling bushes can be pruned back quite hard right into the older wood in April. Always remove the suckers coming up from the base of the bushes. This should be done in July and again, if necessary, in October.

Tamarisk   Can be grown as specimens or as hedges. Specimens should be pruned hard in February, cutting back last year's wood to within 2 in. of its base. Hedges must be pruned hard immediately after flowering.

Tree lupins   Cut away some of the older wood in February and shorten back some of last year's shoots by half.

Weigela   See *Diervilla*.

17 Creepers and climbers

The main rules for pruning shrubs, as given in the previous chapter, hold good for creepers and climbers. However because it is necessary to restrict their growth to a flat surface. certain things have to be done to get the best out of the plants. In the first place, you will usually need to stretch wires tightly along your walls and fences, to which the branches of the shrubs can be tied or on to which the climbers can cling. Some climbing plants, like the virginia creeper, have little clinging tendrils of their own and need no supports at all. I don't advise planting ivies, which not only ruin mortar in between bricks or the woodwork of a fence, but are often also the breeding ground of pests and particularly slugs. Virginia creeper, too, is unsuitable for the walls of a house. Don't, whatever you do, continually knock nails in the walls wherever you want to tie a branch, because in time this can do a tremendous amount of damage to the structure.

Train a shrub or climber carefully from the start with the idea of using it to cover its allotted space. Remember that if it is there to cover 12 ft you must give it that amount of space to spread. If eventually it is to cover a larger area, then it is possible for the time being to use a dwarfer shrub like cotoneaster horizontalis. Remove the cotoneaster later on when the larger-spreading shrub needs to take its place.

In general, far more pruning has to be done to shrubs grown against walls than to those grown as specimens in the border. It is often necessary, for instance, in the early stages to prune back the original long growths quite hard so as to get the plant growing well. Remember that pruning hard back invariably encourages the production of further laterals and leaders and the wall or fence will be covered more quickly as a result. Never be afraid of cutting out the older branches if necessary to make room for the new. Stick to the general rules for pruning all shrubs – in other words aim to prune immediately after flowering.

Here is a list of the principal shrubs and climbers grown in gardens today, with individual instructions as to how each should be pruned. It hasn't been possible to include every kind of shrub or climber, but all the more important ones are dealt with.

Actinidia   Prune in February. Thin out the branches if necessary. Cut back the one-year-old growths to within 1 in. of their base. Reduce by half any straggling growths.

Akebia   These twine and climb almost naturally. Some people leave them alone to grow informally. Others dislike the 'twistiness' this produces and so they thin the growths out. To keep this climber under control in a small space, prune back hard immediately after flowering.

Aristolochia   The simplest method is just to do a little thinning out. On the other hand, if this climber has to grow in a restricted space cut back to within 1 in. of their base all the secondary shoots each late February.

Berchemia   Another twisty type of climber which needs thinning out each early March. Cut out unnecessary growths.

Campsis   In late March or early April cut back the long growths by about one third and prune the side growths to within 3 or 4 in. of their base. Always see that the main branches are spread out well, because it is most important to give the wood a good chance to get thoroughly ripened.

Ceanothus   Most gardeners use the evergreen types for walls and fences and these should be cut back fairly hard immediately after flowering.

Celastrus   Prune immediately the leaves have fallen – cut back the strongest growths by about half and prune the side growths to within 2 or 3 in. of their base.

Ceratostigma   Thin out the branches each early spring so as to keep them spaced out 6–8 in. apart. One variety, *C. willmottianum*, should be pruned hard back each year to within 6 in. or so of its base. It is treated very much like a herbaceous plant and responds to this treatment admirably.

Chimonanthus   This extremely fragrant shrub is often grown as a wall plant in a warm spot. It should be pruned back quite hard immediately flowering is over.

Clematis   Two main types are grown on walls and fences: those that flower on the young wood and those that flower on the old wood.

The young wood flowering types include *C. jackmanii*, *C. aromatica*, *C. paniculata* and *C. viticella*. Cut back to within 2–3 in. of the old wood each winter, only leaving three or four vigorous shoots each season.

*Clematis jackmanii Showing new shoot bearing flower buds growing
from old wood pruned in winter*

The main species that flower on the old wood are *C.
montana*, *C. patens*, *C. florida* and *C. macropetala*,
together, of course, with the various varieties falling
within these species. These should be pruned immediately after flowering, some time early in the summer.

One species, *C. coccinea*, grows very much like a herbaceous plant, dying back each winter and then
sending up new shoots in the spring. Cut out the dead
wood each early February.

Clematis montana Showing flowers on old wood and new shoot developing

Clematis coccinea Herbaceous – last year's growth has been cut to the ground. Next growth shoots up in spring

Cotoneaster   Little pruning is usually necessary but it helps to thin out the branches early in the spring if necessary, and it is always possible to cut back some of the branches to keep them within bounds.

Cydonia japonica   Originally called *pyrus japonica* and now called *chaenomeles japonica*. For pruning, please see page 116.

Escallonia   For pruning see page 117. Remember to tie in the young wood after the old is cut away.

Euonymus   Both the species *radicans* and *japonicus* climb on their own without any help. Prune back at almost any time of the year to keep tidy and in bounds.

Forsythia   For pruning, see page 117.

Garrya   It is seldom necessary to do much pruning. Sometimes a branch or two may have to be cut out immediately after flowering and at other times the young growths may be pruned back to within 1–2 in. of their base. Always tie in after pruning.

Hydrangea   The species *H. petiolaris* is a climber with its own clingers, which means that it needn't be tied in. It is always possible to thin out excess growth and cut back any excessively long shoots late in February.

Jasmine   Prune as advised on page 118.

Lonicera   In the case of the climbing species always cut out the old wood immediately after flowering. At the same time, cut back the strong growths to any point desired.

Magnolia   Often trained against walls. Prune as explained on pages 118–19.

Myrtus   Thin out as necessary every February to keep the branches well apart. The scale insect is a nuisance and if these wall shrubs get overcrowded it is difficult to control this pest.

Polygonum   There are a number of climbing species, the strongest of which is *P. baldschuanicum*. This can be pruned hard each winter, if necessary, and even if it is cut down to within 1 ft of ground level it will always make plenty of growth next spring. The other species should be pruned immediately after flowering with the idea of cutting out the old wood.

Pyracantha   Prune as advised on page 121.

Rose   Divided up into two groups, the ramblers and the climbers.

   Climbers should be pruned in February to cut out all the weak wood and any dead shoots. Aim to train the

branches round and round a post to produce the
maximum number of flowering laterals.

Ramblers should be pruned in August, as a rule the
moment they have finished flowering. Cut down almost
to soil level the growths that have recently bloomed and
tie up the young wood in its place.

Tecoma   Each year prune back the growths in late February
and train any climbing shoots in position so as to give them
plenty of room.

*Wistaria   Showing the long shoots beginning to grow; these must be
shortened in July*

Vitis   This family contains the virginia creeper which, of
course, is a self-clinging species; it can be cut back as
required, and thinned out in the winter if necessary. The
other species of vitis should have their laterals pruned back
late February and if any shoots are needed to take the place
of older growths that have died or need cutting out, some
laterals can be left to act as replacements.

Wistaria   One of the most beautiful of the climbers – and as a
rule one of the worst treated. Each July shorten back the
young laterals to within five buds of their base. Then in
February shorten them back again to within two buds of
their base. This summer and winter pruning results in nice
short spurs bearing plenty of flowering buds. Keep training
out the main shoots to increase the spread of the wistaria,
and continue to cut back the laterals as advised.

Index

Page references in bold type indicate illustrations.

Date Due		
FEB 1 1 1980		
Mar 1/80 MYE		
APR 3 1981 M		
MAY 1 3 1981		
SEP 2 6 1983		
FEB 1 8 1990		
MAR 9 1990		
MAY 1 0 1990		
SEP 1 8 1995		
JUN 1996		

FORM 109